ENCYCLOPAEDIA OF INDIAN GOVERNMENT: PROGRAMMES AND POLICIES

ENCYCLOPAEDIA
OF
INDIAN GOVERNMENT:
PROGRAMMES AND POLICIES

Vol. 14

Power

Potential and Development

Edited by

Satish Tiwari

ANMOL PUBLICATIONS PVT. LTD.

NEW DELHI - 110 002 (INDIA)

ANMOL PUBLICATIONS PVT. LTD.
4374/4B, Ansari Road, Daryaganj
New Delhi - 110 002

Encyclopaedia of Indian Government: Programmes and Policies

First Edition, 2000
ISBN 81-261-0515-1 (Set)

PRINTED IN INDIA

Published by J.L. Kumar for Anmol Publications Pvt. Ltd., New Delhi - 110 002 and Printed at Mehra Offset Press, Delhi.

Contents

Preface

Encyclopaedia of Indian Government: Programmes and Policies contains authoritative information on about fifty departmental policies and their future developmental programmes.

Organised to be completed in 40 volumes, this gigantic work covers Agriculture; Atomic Energy; Chemicals and Fertilizers; Coal; Commerce; Communication; Culture; Defence; Education; Environment and Forests; External Affairs; Finance; Food & Consumer Affairs; Food Processing Industries; Health and Family Welfare; Home Affairs and Internal Security; Human Resources; Industry; Information and Broadcasting; Labour; Law, Justice and Company Affairs; Non-conventional Energy Sources; Ocean Development; Parliamentary Affairs; Personnel, Public Grievances and Pensions; Petroleum and Natural Gas; Planning and Programme Implementation; Planning and Statistics; Posts and Telegraphs; Power; Rural Development; Science and Technology; Social Justice and Empowerment; Space; States Affairs; Steel; Steel and Mines; Sugar and Edible Oils; Surface Transport; Textiles; Tourism; Urban Development; Water Resources; Women and Child development etc.

Based on the information derived from authoritative sources, this work contains authentic facts and figures. I am deeply beholden to all the scholars whose writings are cited or substantially made use of in the present work. I am also thankful to Anmol Publications Pvt. Ltd. for undertaking publication of this encyclopaedia. I am solely responsible for shortcomings in presentation of matter.

Encyclopaedic in nature, this will prove a dependable reference work for scholars and academics besides those appearing for different competitive examinations.

—Satish Tiwari

1

Ministry of Power

The Ministry of Power started functioning independently with effect from 2nd July, 1992. Earlier it was known as the Ministry of Energy comprising the Department of Power, Coal and Non-Conventional Energy Sources.

Electricity is a concurrent subject at Entry 38 in List III of the Seventh Schedule of the Constitution of India. The Ministry of Power is primarily responsible for the development of electrical energy in the country. The Ministry is concerned with perspective planning, policy formulation, processing of projects for investment decision, monitoring of the implementation of power projects, training and manpower development and the administration and enactment of legislation in regard to thermal, hydel power generation, transmission and distribution.

The Ministry of Power is responsible for the administration of the Indian Electricity Act, 1910 and Electricity (Supply) Act, 1948, Electricity Regulatory Commission Act. 1998 and to undertake such amendments to these Acts, as may be necessary from time to time, in conformity with the Government's policy objectives.

The Ministry of Power is mainly responsible for evolving general policy in the field of energy. The main items of work dealt with by the Ministry of Power are as below:

— General Policy in the Electric Power Sector and issues relating to energy policy. (Details of short, medium and long-term policies in terms of formulation, acceptance, implementation and review of such policies, cutting across sectors, fuels, regions and cross country flows).

— All matters relating to hydro-electric power (except mini micro hydel projects of and below 25 MW capacity and Geo-thermal energy) and thermal power and transmission System Network.

— Research, development and technical-assistance relating to hydro-electric and thermal power and transmission system network.

— Administration of the Indian Electricity Act, 1910 (9 of 1910) and the Electricity (Supply) Act, 1948(54 of 1948)/ERC Act 1998.

— All matters relating to Central Electricity authority, Central Electricity Board and Central Electricity Regulatory Commission.

— Rural Electrification, power schemes in Union territories and issues relating to power supply in the States and Union territories.

— Matters relating to the following Undertakings/ Organisations etc:

(a) The Damodar Valley Corporation.

(b) Bhakra Beas Management Board (except irrigation matters).

(c) National Thermal Power Corporation Limited.

(d) National Hydro-electric Power Corporation Limited.

(e) Rural Electrification Corporation Limited.

(f) North Eastern Electric Power Corporation Limited.

(g) Power Grid Corporation of India Limited.

(h) Power Finance Corporation Limited.

(i) Tehri Hydro Development Corporation.

(j) Nathpa Jhakri Power Corporation.

(k) Central Power Research Institute.

(l) National Power Training Institute.

(m) Energy Management Centre.

— Other Public Sector Enterprises concerned with the subject included under this Department except such projects as are specifically allotted to any other Ministry/Department.

— All matters concerning Energy Conservation and Energy Efficiency pertaining to Power sector.

Organisations under ministry of power

In all technical and economic matters, Ministry of Power is assisted by the Central Electricity Authority (CEA) constituted under the Electricity (Supply) Act, 1948.

Badarpur Management Contract Cell (BMCC), a sobordinate office of this Ministry, is responsible for administering the Badarpur Thermal Power Station (BTPS) Management Contract between the Government of India and NTPC.

The construction and operation of generation and transmission projects in the Central Sector are entrusted to Central Sector Power Corportions, viz. The National Thermal Power Corporation (NTPC), the National Hydro Electric Power Corporation (NHPC), the North Eastern Electric Power Corporation (NEEPCO) and the Power Grid Corporation of India Limited (PGCIL) The

Powergrid is responsible for all the existing and future transmission projects in the Central Sector and also for the formation of the National Power Grid.

Two Joint Venture Power Corporations namely, Nathpa Jhakri Power Corporation (NJPC) and Tehri Hydro Development Corporation (THDC) are responsible for the execution of the Nathpa Jhakri Power Project in Himachal Pradesh and projects of the Tehri Hydro Power Complex in Uttar Pradesh respectively. Two statutory bodies i.e., the Damodar Valley Corporation (DVC) and the Bhakra Beas Management Board (BBMB) are also under the administrative control of the Ministry of Power. Programmes of Rural electrification are provided financial assistance by the Rural Electrification Corporation (REC) under the Ministry of Power.

The Power Finance Corporation (PFC) provides termfinance to projects in the power sector. Further, the autonomous bodies (societies) i.e., Central Power Research Institute (CPRI), the National Power Training Institute (NPTI) and the Energy Management Centre (EMC) are also under the administrative control of the Ministry of Power.

Organisational set-up

Shri P. R. Kumaramangalam, is the Minister of Power with effect from 19.03.1998. He is also holding the portfolio of Minister-in-charge of Parliamentary Affairs and Ministry of Non-Conventional Energy Sources w.e.f 30.1.1999 and 3.2.1999 respectively. Dr. E. A. S. Sarma was the Secretary(Power) upto 03.07.1998. Shri V. K. Pandit took over as Secretary(Power) on 04.07.1998. He is assisted by a Special Secretary and Six Joint Secretaries, including the Financial Adviser. There are six Wings in the Ministry of Power, each headed by a Joint secretary. These are:

— Administration; Systems; Energy Conservation; Co-ordination; 'Rural Electrification and Vigilance & Security.

— Thermal and Operation Monitoring.

— Investment Promotion and Power Finance Corporation.

— Hydel

— Policy Planning & External Assistance and Reforms & Restructuring.

— Internal Finance.

There is a Principal Accounts Office headed by Controller of Accounts who in turn reports to Financial Adviser in the Ministry of Power. Matter relating to reservations of SC/ST are dealt by SC/ST Cell whereas reservation for Physically Handicapped is dealt with in Coordination Division of the Ministry of Power. The total staff strength of the Ministry is 313.

Central electricity regulatory

The Central Electricity Regulatory Commission (CERC), an independent statutory body with quasi-judicial powers, has been constituted on 25th July, 1998 under the Electricity Regulatory Commission Act, 1998. The Commission consists of a Chairperson and four other Members including the Chairman, CEA as the ex-officio member. Prof. S.L. Rao, formerly DG, National Council of Applied Economics Research (NCAER) and Shri D.P. Sinha, Shri G.S. Rajamani and Shri A.R. Ramanathan have assumed charge as Chairperson and as Members, Engineering, Finance & Law respectively.

The functions of the Commission are :

— To regulate the tariff of generating companies owned or controlled by the Central Government;

— To regulate inter-State transmission including tariff of the transmission entities;

— To promote competition, efficiency and economy in the sector;

— To regulate inter-State bulk sale of power;

— To aid and advise the Central Government in formulation of tariff policy and to frame guidelines relating to electricity tariff;

— To associate with the environmental regulatory agencies towards developing policies and procedures for environmental regulations for the power sector;

— To arbitrate or adjudicate in matters relating to tariff.

CERC has drafted the regulations relating to conduct of business which includes matters relating to tariff. Comments have been invited on this draft from the members of the public through advertisements in the national newspapers on 07.12.1998.

2

Highlights and Main Achievements

Power generation

The overall generation in the country has increased from 287 BUs during 1991-92 to 420 BUs during 1997-98.

The yearwise generation is as follows

Year	Generation (BUs)
1991-92	287
1992-93	301
1993-94	324
1994-95	351
1995-96	380
1996-97	394
1997-98	420
1998-99 (Apr '98—Jan'99)	369.4
1998-99 (Apr '98—Mar '99)	450

Installed capacity

The All India Installed Capacity of electric power generating stations under utilities was 89166.87 MW as of 31.3.98 consisting of 21891.08 MW Hydro, 64150.78 MW Thermal and 2225 MW Nuclear and 900.01 MW Wind which has increased to 91066.18 MW (Statement-1) as on 31.1.99 consisting of 22083.08 MW Hydro 65789.98 MW

Thermal and 2225.00 (prov.) MW Nuclear and 968.12 MW Wind. At present the rerated installed nuclear capacity is 1840 MW.

Capacity addition during 1997-98

As against the Capacity addition programme of 3239 MW for the year 1997-98, a capacity of 3283.3 MW was achieved. Though a capacity of 860 MW had slipped the same was compensated by addition of 904.3 MW from outside the programme (i e. units not anticipated in the beginning) . As against the capacity addition target of 516 MW in hydel and 2725 MW in thermal, a capacity of 233 MW and 3050.3 MW respectively was achieved.

Capacity addition during 1998-99

A capacity addition programme of 3299.30 MW consisting of 544.50 MW of Hydro and 2754.80 MW of thermal has been envisaged for the year 1998-99. As against the afford said capacity addition target the capacity of 1556.20 MW consisting of 192MW of hydro and 1364.20 MW of thermal has been achieved up to 31.1.99.

Ninth plan capacity addition programme

The draft 9th Plan prepared by the Planning Commission envisages a total capacity addition of 40245.2 MW comprising 9819.7 MW hydro, 29545.5 MW thermal and 880 MW nuclear power. The sector wise and regionwise additions proposed are as follows:

Sectorwise Benefits (MW)

Sector	Hydro	Thermal	Nuclear	Total
Central	3455.0	7574.0	880.0	11909.0
State	5814.7	4933.0	-	10747.7
Private	550.0	17038.5	-	17588.5
Total	9819.7	29545.5	880.0	40245.2

Regionwise Benefits (MW)

Region	Hydro	Thermal	Nuclear	Total
Northern	4177.0	3360.0	440.0	7977.0
Western	2212.5	8361.7	—	10574.2
Southern	1824.5	7684.3	440.0	9948.8
Eastern	918.5	3890.0	—	4808.8
N.E. Region	682.0	229.5	—	911.5
A & N Island	5.2	20.0	—	25.2
Total	9819.7	23545.0	880.0	34245.2
Liquid Fuel	—	6000.0	—	6000.0
All India	9819.7	29545.5	880.0	40245.2

The Planning Commission has provided an outlay of Rs. 46143.66 crore in the Central Sector for the Ninth Plan.

Plant load factor (PLF)

The actual all India PLF of Thermal Utilities during April 98 to Jan. 1999 was 63.3% which was 1.0% less than the target of 64.3% for this period.

The PLF figures during the last five years and April 1998 to Jan. 99 are as under:

(Figures in %)

Year	Centre	State	Overall
1993-94	69.8	56.6	61.0
1994-95	69.2	55.0	60.0
1995-96	71.0	58.1	63.0
1996-97	71.1	60.3	64.4
1997-98	70.4	60.9	64.7
1998-99	69.0	59.6	63.3

A target of 65.7% has been fixed for the year 1998-99.

Transmission & distribution losses

The T&D losses in the country are on the higher side. The T&D losses in the country, due to concerted efforts has come down from 22.83% during the year 1991-92 to 21.13% in 1994-95 resulting in a reduction of 1.70%. However, there has been an increase in losses thereafter in the years 1995-96 and 1996-97.

The yearwise details of the T&D losses for the last four years are given below:

Year	T&D Losses (%)
1993-94	21.41%
1994-95	21.13%
1995-96	22.27%
1996-97	23.41%

Power supply position

The power supply position during the last five years and during the current year (April '98 - Jan. '99) has been as under:-

Energy (MU net)

Year	Requirement	Availability	Shortage	
			Total	(%)
1993-94	323252	299494	23758	7.3
1994-95	352260	327281	24979	7.1
199596	389721	354045	35676	9.2
1996-97	413490	365900	47590	11.5
1997-98	424505	390330	34175	8.1
1998-99	368046	347900	20146	5.5

(April '98 - Jan.'99)

Year	Peak Demand	Peak Met	Deficit	Shortage (%)
1993-94	54875	44830	10045	18.3
1994.95	57530	48066	9464	16.5
1995-96	60981	49836	11145	18.3
1996-97	63853	52376	11477	18.0
1997-98	65435	58042	7393	11.3
1998-99	65956	58636	7320	11.1
(April '98 - Jan.'99)				

It may be seen that the energy shortage has been reducing gradually and during the year 98-99 it has reduced to 5.5%. The peak shortage during the year 98-99 (April '98 - Jan.'99) has been a little lower than last year.

Restructuring of state electricity boards

— Presently restructuring and regulatory reforms are contemplated with a view to bring about reforms in the SEBs through establishment of State Electricity Regulatory Commissions.

— The establishment of Regulatory Commissions, as provided in the Act passed by the Parliament, would lead to rationalisation of tariff and also provide for transparency in the provisional subsidies, whereever required. The State Government can provide the option of providing subsidies, over and above, those reco-mmended by the Regulatory Commissions, on condition that the State Governments compensate the SEBs by providing adequate budgetary support. When tariffs are rationalised and budgetary support is provided, SEBs will improve their financial positions.

— The Government of Orissa has already introduced reform programmes by setting up Orissa State Electricity Regulatory Commission, Orissa generating company having thermal units under it, Orissa Hydro Electric Generating company and Grid Corporation of Orissa. Haryana Government has also initiated reforms programmes by unbundling of SEB into corporations and setting up of Electricity Regulatory Commission. Andhra Pradesh has also introduced reforms.

— The Governments of Andhra Pradesh, Uttar Pradesh, Rajasthan, Madhya Pradesh and Goa have already referred their proposals for setting up independent regulatory mechanism in their states. The Government of Karnataka is the first to invite Private Sector participation in transmission by setting up Joint Venture company. Other states are also in the process of introducing reforms.

State electricity boards-rate of return

Restoration of financial health of SEBs and improvement in their Operational performance continue to remain a critical issue in the power sector. In terms of section 59 of the Electricity (supply) Act 1948, SEBs are required to achieve a rate of return (ROR) of not less than 3 percent on their fixed assets in service at the beginning of the year after providing for interest and depreciation charges less consumer's contribution. This provision has become operative from the accounting year 1985. While in 1993-94,14 SEBs out of 17 SEBs (including OSEB) had a positive ROR (including subsidy), in 1996-97 13 SEBs out of 16 SEBs (excluding OSEB) had a positive ROR (including subsidy). Further only 4 SEBs (MSEB, HPSEB, PSEB & TNEB) had a ROR of more than 3 percent in 1996-97 (with subsidy). Managerial and financial inefficiencies in state sector utilities have adversely affected capacity addition and system improvement. While the SEBs do not have enough resources to finance future programmes they are also unable to raise investible funds from alternate sources due to their poor financial and commercial performance.

Sixteenth electric power survey committee

The sixteenth Electric Power Survey Committee was consituted by the Central Electricity Authority in March, 1998 with Member (Planning), Central Electricity Authority as its Chairman. The terms of reference of the Committee are - to review the demand projections for each State and Union Territory in detail upto the year 2004-05 and project the perspective demand upto the year 2014-15. Two meetings of the 16th EPS Committee had been held in the current year. The work is in progress.

Conference of chief ministers on power

The Chief Ministers/Power Ministers met on 18th December, 1998 to discuss and deliberate upon the critical issues pertaining to the power sector. Recognising that significant changes have taken place in India's power sector after the adoption of the Common Minimum National Action Plan for Power, it was decided that a new initiative needs to be taken to move India's power sector into the next phase of reforms. It was concluded that reform of the power sector is essential not only to facilitate additional investments but also improve the availability of reasonably priced power to the common man. With this end in view, the following plan of action was adopted for implementation:

— *State Electricity Regulatory Commissions*: Each State/ Union Territory shall constitute SERC before 31st March, 1999 to enable rationalisation of tariffs and improvement of the financial health of State Electricity Boards and to avail the interest subsidy on loans by the Power Finance Corporation as well as other incentives available.

— *Power Sector Reform Bill* Orissa, Haryana and Andhra Pradesh have already enacted the Reforms Bills outlining a reform plan for their power sectors. Each State/Union Territory shall announce a power sector reform policy and initiate steps for drawing up a Reform Bill wherever necessary in a time bound manner.

— *Corporatisation* State/Union Territories will endeavour to take steps to corporatise and commercialise generating companies, transmission companies and distribution companies so that they are able to operate on commercial principles, generate the required resources and ensure availability of reasonably priced power to the common man.

— *Distribution Reforms* In view of the urgent need to reduce transmission and distribution losses, facilitate higher investments in system improvement and ensure availability of reliable power to the consumers, reform of the distribution sector will be initiated by establishing distribution companies in different regions of each State. The entry of private investors will be encouraged wherever feasible. To begin with, at least 25% of the State will be taken up for distribution reform. The whole State will be covered in 4 years.

— *Mega Projects* To take advantage of the benefits of mega projects, each State/Union Territory will take steps to facilitate setting up of mega projects in accordance with the guidelines issued by Govt. of India.

— *Commercial arrangements for payment for power* Having

regard to the large investments required to be undertaken by CPSUs for generation and transmission projects, State/Union Territories will adopt commercial arrangements such as opening of LCs of the required amount for payment of power from generating and transmission agencies and for prompt settlement of dues.

— *Securitisation* To enable CPSUs to take up new projects for generation and transmission and in accordance with the Government of India policy of securitisation of the outstanding debts of Central Public Sector Undertakings, State Governments will take steps to facilitate orderly securitisation of such debts.

— *Hydel Projects* Recognising the need for expeditious development of hydel potential in the country, the State Governments will take necessary steps (i) to complete languishing projects, (ii) and to take up the execution of hydroelectric projects by resolving outstanding inter-State issues. The State Governments will also provide assistance to the CPSUs in acquiring land and other clearances/ approvals to take up the execution of the hydel projects in the Central Sector for benefits in the 10th Plan (2002-2007).

— *National Power Grid* Keeping in view the imperative need to speedily develop a National Power Grid with appropriate transmission linkages at the state level for optimum utilisation of available generation within the various regions, the Central and State Sectors will substantially step up investment in transmission to complete the critical transmission lines and overcome the present mismatch in investment between generation and transmission of power.

— *Energy Conservation* Realising the need to conserve energy, each State/ Union Territory will formulate and launch an Action Plan for energy conservation. Government of India will introduce an Energy Conservation Bill in Parliament shortly.

— *Increase in Power Generation* In order to increase power generation quickly and reduce power shortages, at least ten power projects will be enabled to achieve financial closure and start construction by March 1999.

— *Electricity Tariff for Railways* Realising the need to maintain viability of Railways and State Electricity Boards, it will be the endeavour of the State Governments to rationalise Railway Tariff. Simultaneously, the Railway Ministry would look into and rationalise the cost structure of Coal movement for Power projects.

Development/ new initiatives in the power sector

The Electricity Regulatory Commissions Ordinance was promulgated on 25th April, 1998 with a view to providing for the establishment of the Central Electricity Regulatory Commission and State Electricity Regulatory Commissions, rationalisation of electricity tariffs, transparent policies regarding subsidies, promotion of efficient and environmentally benign policies and for matters connected therewith and incidental thereto. The Ordinance has since been replaced by an Act (No.14 of 1998) of Parliament with certain amendments. The amendments pertain to Sections 17 (1), 29(3) and subsequent change in Section 51 of the Ordiance.

The Government has constituted Central Electricity Regulatory Commission (CERC) under the provisions of the Act. Shri S.L. Rao, former Director General, NCAER, has taken over as Chairperson and Shri A.R.

Ramanathan, former Member of Company Law Board, Shri D.P. Sinha and Shri G.S. Rajamani, former Members of the Central Electricity Authority have taken over as Members of the Central Commission.

The main functions of CERC are to regulate the tariff of generating companies owned or controlled by the Central Government, to regulate inter-State transmission including tariff of the transmission entities, to regulate inter-State bulk sale of power, to aid and advise the Central Government in formulation of tariff policy, etc.

State electricity regulatory commissions

Orissa and Haryana have set up SERCs under the State Reforms Act. Andhra Pradesh has made a provision for creation of SERC under the Andhra Pradesh Electricity Reforms Act and is in the process of finalising selection for Chairperson and Members of the Commission. States like Madhya Pradesh, Uttar Pradesh, Arunachal Pradesh, West Bengal and Gujarat have notified constitution of the SERCs under the Central Act. Some other States like Tamilnadu, Rajasthan and Maharashtra have constituted Selection Committees for selection of Chairman and Members of the SERCs.

State reforms acts

Several State Governments have taken concrete steps towards power sector reforms. States like Orissa, Haryana and Andhra Pradesh have passed the Reforms Bill in their respective States. Karnataka has drafted the State Reforms Ordinance. Uttar Pradesh has also

Unbundling of activities of SEBs

States of Orissa, Haryana and Andhra Pradesh have unbundled the activities of their respective SEBs. The State of Orissa has unbundled generation, transmission and distribution into separate entities by setting up Orissa Power Generation Corporation (Genco), Orissa

Hydro Power Corporation (OHPC) and Grid Corporation of Orissa Limited (Gridco). In Haryana, generation, transmission and distribution activities of State Electricity Board have been corporatised into separate companies. As regards distribution, the State has been divided into two distribution zones - Northern and Southern. The two distribution companies namely Uttar Vidyut Vitaran Nigam Limited and Dakshin Vidyut Vitaran Nigam Limited have been formed for the two zones. Andhra Pradesh has set up under the AP Electricity Reforms Act, two corporations namely Transmission Corporation of Andhra Pradesh Limited (APTRANSCO) and Andhra Pradesh Power Generation Limited (APGENCO) in place of APSEB.

Task force for monitoring reforms and restructuring in states

Task force under the chairmanship of Secretary (Power) has been set up to monitor the progress of reforms in various states.

Energy conservation

A proposal has been formulated for enactment of an enabling legislation on energy conservation giving the Central government and State Governments the requisite statutory powers for promoting and enforcing a progressive regime of energy conservation in the country. For operationalising the concepts contained in the proposed legislation, a Bureau of Energy Efficiency (BEE) is proposed to be set up.

Energy conservation is proposed to be attained through setting up of energy conservation standards for any equipment or appliance consuming, generating, transmitting or supplying energy. There shall be a scheme for compulsory affixing of labels on notified equipment and appliances and certain industries, establishments and users of energy shall be notified as designated consumers, keeping in view the intensity and quantity of energy consumption. As and when required by the designated authority, energy audit by an a credited auditor shall be mandatory for all designated consumers. Energy Managers with prescribed qualifications may be required to be appointed by the designated consumers.

Such designated consumers would be required to submit a report on the status of energy conservation to the BEE on an annual basis. The BEE would prepare guidelines for building codes relating to energy conservation. Codes could be modified to suit local climatic conditions. Energy audit of specific designated consumers in respect of buildings could also be prescribed.

The State Governments may, in consultation with BEE, designate one or more agencies to coordinate, enforce and regulate matters relating to the implementation of the legislation within the State. It is proposed that the State and Central Governments and their designated agencies shall promote mass awareness for energy conservation, consumer education and consumer guidance. The Government shall also take steps to encourage preferential treatment for energy efficient equipment and appliances.

The proposed bill also provides for constitution of an Energy Conservation Fund at the Centre and the State level for utilising any grant or loans made available for promoting energy conservation.

The Bureau is expected to be set up without any substantial creation of new posts. The existing Energy Management Centre under Ministry of Power is proposed to be merged with the Bureau of Energy Efficiency with suitable restructuring.

Amendment to acts

— The Government of India in the Ministry of Power have enacted Electricity Regulatory Commissions Act, 1998 for establishment of Central Electricity Regulatory Commission (CERC) at the national level and SERCs in States for rationalisation of tariffs and matters related thereto. The CERC has been set up on 24-7-1998. It is now for the States to restructure the power sector under the provisions of this Act. The progress made in the States is being monitored.

— Electricity Amendment Act, 1998: Transmission has been made a separate activity which would help in inviting greater participation in investment both from the public and private sector. The guidelines in this regard are under finalisation.

— Energy Conservation: The need for amendments in this area have been examined and the Bill on Energy Conservation is being finalised for introduction in the Parliament.

— Existing Indian Electricity Act, 1910 and Electricity (Supply) Act, 1948 have been reviewed and it has been decided that it would not be appropriate to go for changes in them at this stage.

— Electricity Development fund: Under the policy on hydro-power development, it has been proposed to levy access of 5 paise per Kwh on electricity generated in the country for maintaining a separate Electricity Development Fund for the purposes of utilising the amount for taking up survey and investigation preparation of DPRs and the construction activities of hydel projects. The Fund will also be used for promoting new hydel projects including small hydel projects and for improvement in transmission/distribution network including sub-transmission and distribution. The necessary legislation for the purpose is being drafted and will be introduced in the Parliament.

— Privatisation of distribution: It is for the State Governments to take initiatives in this regard and also For the unbundling of SEBs into separate activities for generation, transmission and distribution by enactment of necessary laws. The model law in this regard was circulated to all the States as a part of agenda for the Chief Ministers Conference held on 18th Dec., 1998.

Private participation in transmission

After the recent amendment in Electricity Laws, transmission activity has been given an independent status and the concept of Central and State transmission utilities has been introduced. While POWERGRID has been notified as the Central Transmission Utility (CTU), the State Electricity Boards or their successor State transmission companies would be the State transmission utilities. It is mandated in the Act that CTU and STU would be Government companies.

The participation by Private Sector in the area of transmission is proposed to be limited to construction and maintenance of transmission lines for operation under the supervision and control of CTU/STU.

The process would involve identification of transmission lines by the CTU/STU to be entrusted to Private Sector, issue of specifications, calling for offers and selection of the private party. On selection of the private company, the CTU/STU would recommend to the CERC/SERC for issuance of a transmission licence to the private company.

The private company shall contract only with the CTU/STU for the entire use of the transmission line(s) constructed by the company, and shall be responsible for the maintenance of the lines. Transmission charges payable to the company would be directly linked to the availability of the lines. The guidelines for Private Sector participation have been prepared.

Special programmes for development of north east and J&K

The Government had earlier announced new initiatives for North-Eastern region and J&K State in order to improve the power situation and bring about overall development of the areas. As a follow-up measure, the Ministry of Power is constantly reviewing the projects included in the package programme announced by the Prime Minister during the year 1996.

A high level team consisting of officers from Ministry of Power and CEA visited J&K in June, 98 and January, 99 for review of activities relating to Power Sector. As a result of such reviews the power situation in J&K has considerably improved. The transmission facilities in J&K have also been strengthened. Quarterly Reports on the progress are being sent to the J&K Department in the Ministry of Home Affairs regularly. Ministry of Power has also drawn up an Action Plan for the development of the North Eastern region encompassing capacity addition programme as well as strengthening transmission lines and strengthening the sub-transmission and distribution system.

Meritorious productivity and incentive awards

The Meritorious Productivity Award Scheme is awarded to Thermal Power Stations based on their P.L.F. This scheme was introduced in the year 1983-84. It envisages cash award to power stations' personnel for excellence in productivity. In addition to this, shields are awarded to stations exceeding specified levels of generation and medals (Gold, Silver & Bronze) are awarded to General

Manager/Chief Engineer/Head of the power station as per the performance of their stations.

Another scheme was introduced from Calendar Year 1992 for thermal power stations for achieving economic and efficient performance. Under this scheme power stations which achieve more than a specified improvement in their secondary fuel oil consumption and Auxilliary Power Consumption as compared to that of previous year would be given cash awards by the Government.

3

Transmission

Transmission projects continue to be accorded a high priority in the context of the need to evacuate power from the generating stations to the load centres. The transmission works construction programme for the year 1998-99 in the country and the progress achieved during the year 1998-99 (upto Nov '98) in the construction of transmission lines and substations for 220 kV and above) is summarised below:

Works	Programme 1998-99 (ckm)	Achievement April '98-Nov (ckm)
+/- 500 kV		
HVDC lines	1135	1119
800 kV lines	405	291
400 kV lines	3004	1346
220 kV lines	3210	2380
400 kV substations (Nos.)	2205	945
220 kV substations (Nos.)	4890	3400

Central sector transmission

Central sector transmission works completed during the year 1998-99 (upto Nov. 98) are listed in the following table:-

Name of Transmission Work	Voltage (kv)	Length (ckm)
1. Bongaigaon-Siliguri	400 D/C	440
2. Ranganadi-Balipara	400 D/C	333
3. Jeypore-Gazuwaka	400 D/C	442
4. Kopili-Misa	220 S/C	76
5. Kayamkulam-Edamon	220 D/C	156

At the time of fourth Five Year Plan several inter-state and inter-regional transmission lines were planned to facilitate the integrated operation of the state systems within the region. Loan assistance equivalent to the full cost of the scheme is extended to the state governments under the centrally sponsored programme for construction of such inter-state lines.

Upto the end of the financial year 1997-98, a cumulative sum of Rs. 36190-25 lakh was released to the states under the programme stringing of over 7000 ckm of 66 kV and above transmission lines have been completed.

For the year 1998-99, the approved budget provision for relasing loan to utilities for centrally sponsored interstate transmission lines is Rs. 170 lakh. Also a loan of Rs. 425.65 lakh during 1998-99 and an outlay of Rs. 179.50 lakh have been proposed for the programme for 1999-2000.

National power grid

The Union Cabinet in 1980 approved in principle the establishment of a centrally owned and operated power grid. The National Power Grid would eventually comprise strong regional network with suitable asynchronous (HVDC) links between the regions. Already 25954 ckm of 400 kV lines and 7374 ckm of 220 kV lines have been constructed in the central sector upto November'98. The inter-regional links of Vindhyachal-Singrauli 400 kV double circuit line with 2x250 MW HVDC back to back at Vindhyachal connecting NR & WR and Chandrapur-Ramagundam 400 kV double circuit line with 2x500 MW HVIDC back to back at Chandrapur-connecting WR & SR is in commercial operation. These as well as other AC links between regions form the important components of the National Power Grid today.

In Oct '89 Government of India established the Powergrid Corporation of India Limited to further accelerate the development of the National Power Grid. Powergrid had already taken over most of the existing central sector transmission systems. Powergrid also proposes to take up schemes for further strengthening of the Regional Powergrids and establish HVIDC B/B inter-regional links. The 400 kV double circuit line between Jeypore (Orissa)-Gazuwaka (Andhra Pradesh) with 1×500 MW HVDC back to back system at Gazuwaka between ER & SR is planned to be completed in the year of 1998-99.

Although the Regional Grids have already been inter connected, paving way for formation of a National Power Grid, further strengthening of intra-regional and inter-regional tie lines would be needed to enable increased power exchanges and achieve improved economy and reliability. This is a continuous process and projects are being taken up during each plan period depending upon the requirement of inter-regional power exchanges and the funds availability.

National high voltage direct current (HVDC) project

The first stage of HVIDC project between Lower Sileru (AP) and Barsoor (MP) was commissioned in October, 1989 with total indigenous know-how. It has been in continuous operation and is presently carrying 20-30 MW power. The second stage of uprating the link to 200 MW + 200 kV was approved in September 1993 at a cost of Rs. 103.98 crore (since revised to Rs. 95.40 crore). The works are in progress and 95% of the equipment are at site. Work at Lower Sileru and Barsoor is completed. Converter Transformer at Lower Sileru have been charged.

The third stage which envisages addition of another pole to convert the monopole DC system to a bipole operation with a voltage level of ± 200 kV DC and power transfer level of 400 MW will be taken after completion of Stage-II.

Flexible AC transmission system

The Flexible AC Transmission System (FACTS) technology is intended to improve the dynamic performance of the power transmission system and achieve regulated power flow across AC transmission network. In order to consider the various aspects of development of flexible AC transmission technology in India, a Committee of Experts under the Chairmanship of Chairman, CEA has been constituted.

The Committee held several meetings and a consensus on the project for implementation of FACTS has been arrived at. Based on this decision BHEL have now prepared a detailed feasibility report for the Flexible AC Transmission Project which envisages installation of Thyristor Controlled Series Compensation (TCSC) on the 400 kV Kanpur Ballabhgarh line of PowerGrid.

The project is scheduled for implementation in 2 stages with a total investment of Rs. 20 crore. Stage-I covering the installation of fixed Series Capacitor (35%) and Stage 11 covering implementing the Variable Series Compensation Scheme (20%) along with necessary controllers.

Shunt capacitors

In order to facilitate transfer of adequate quantum of surplus power from neighbouring region to Southern Region a requirement for installation of 4046 MVAR of shunt capacitors during 1997-98 has been projected. Against this only 1276 MVAR of shunt capacitors have been installed upto Nov. 98. POWERGRID had agreed to procure and install shunt capacitors at SEBs substations on a no-profit no-loss basis. After commissioning of HVDC station at Gazuwaka in March, 1998, it would be possible to transfer 600 MW from Eastern Region, if the system constraints are removed by installing shunt capacitors.

Agreement between POWERGRID & SEBs of Nothern Region for installation of shunt capacitors on the substations of SEBs by POWERGRID was finalised. Goa Electricity Department and Kerala SEB have also agreed to take the assistance of POWERGRID for installation of 100 MVAR & 200 MVAR respectively.

Integrated grid operation

The Regional Power Grids in the Northern, Western, Southern, Eastern and North-Eastern Regions of the country have been established to make optimum utilisation of the unevenly distributed power resources in the country by facilitating flow of power within the Region and exchanges between different Regions to the extent feasible depending upon day to day availability and load conditions.

During 1998-99 all the constituent systems in the Northern, Western, Southern, Eastern and North-Eastern Regions were by and large operating in parallel. Power transfers between Northern Region and Western Region took place asynchronously over Vindhyachal-Singrauli HVDC back-to-back link in both the directions depending on surplus deficit in the two regions. Madhya Pradesh in Western Region received considerable assistance in radial mode from Northern Region over Auraiya Mehgaon line. Andhra Pradesh, Tamil Nadu & Kerala in Southern Region, Madhya Pradesh, Goa, Daman & Diu and Dadra & Nagar Haveli in Western Region and Assam in North-Eastern Region received considerable assistance from NTPC stations in Eastern Region. Besides, Tamil Nadu also availed assistance from Punjab for some period. Southern Region availed off-peak surplus power from Western Region. Karnataka in Southern Region availed assistance in radial mode from Maharashtra under a bilateral arrangement. A part of North Eastern system consisting of lower Assam, Meghalaya, under a bilateral arrangement, A part of North Eastern system consisting of lower Assam, Meghalaya, part of Tripura, Manipur, Mizoram, Arunachal Pradesh, Loktak HEP and NEEPCO's generating stations operated in parallel with Eastern Region throughout the year. Efforts were, therefore, made to maximize the intra and inter regional exchange of energy to the extent possible.

Arrangements were made to maximize power transfer from Eastern Region to Western Region. lb Thermal Power Station and Hirakund Hydro Electric Project along with part of load of GRIDCO system were separated from Eastern Regional Grid and synchronised with Western Regional Grid. With this arrangement power of the order of 300 MW has been transferred from Eastern Region to Western Region, as against 100-150 MW possible in radial arrangement.

System studies were carried out to examine the arrangements required for transfer of power to Andhra Pradesh on 400 kV Jeypore-Gazuwaka line along with 500 MW HVDC back-to-back station at Gazuwaka which is likely to be completed in March, 1999. Strengthening of transmission system required in Andhra Pradesh as well as the capacitor installation requirement in various state systems of Soutern Region were indentified.

Wheeling charges for all the inter-regional transfer of power were worked out based on the recommendations of a Working Group set up by Chairman, CEA comprising representatives of CEA, NTPC, NHDC, POWERGRID and one or two states from each region.

A committee under Member (Power System), CEA comprising representatives of CEA, NTPC & POWERGRID was formed on Trans-Regional Export of surplus of Eastern Region Power. The committee has since submitted its report along with a time bound action plan. The implementation of the recommendations of the committee is being monitored.

Monitoring of system frequency tie line flows, maximization of inter-state inter-regional exchange of power, proper allocation of shares to the beneficiary states systems from Central Sector generation joint projects daily/monthly scheduling of generation, preparation of Load-Generation balance reports including coordination of annual maintenance capital overhauling of generating units, energy accounting on daily basis, energy accounting on monthly basis for billing purpose, facilitation of commercial arrangements for inter-utility trading of power and formulation of policies for safe, secure and economic operation of the Regional Grid were some of the import functions carried out by the Secretariats of the five REBs.

Awards for reduction in T&D Losses

Under the Incentive Scheme, launched by the Govt. of India in the year 1987-88, the SEBs/EDs and their Distribution Divisions/Cities/Towns are awarded with shields on the basis of their performance in reduction of

T&D losses. Cash awards are given to Distribution Divisions/Cities/Towns of the power utilities which achieve a prescribed minimum reduction in T&D losses, individuals as well as institutions and organisations also qualify for grant of incentive for developing scientific devices or presenting new ideas which prove to be effective in saving energy by optimal utilisation of T&D system or better quality of power supply or improved efficiency of electrical appliances.

Import of power from Pakistan

Ministry of Water & Power, Government of Pakistan in its preliminary report submitted to ADB, offered a minimum of 1000 MW going upto 2000 MW during peak period of its surplus power for export to India. A Technical Team was constitued by the Ministry of Power in October, 98 comprising representatives from Ministry of Power, Ministry of External Affairs, Ministry of Finance, Central Electricity Authority, Powergrid and Punjab State Electricity Board in order to examine various aspects for import of power from Pakistan. The Technical Team under the leadership of Special Secretary (Power) visited Pakistan for discussion with Pakistan authorities in the last week of October, 1998.

Pakistan has indicated availability of surplus power upto 2000 MW which could be exported to India at least till the year 2010 and possibly even beyond. A high level five member Pakistani delegation led by Mr. Sayed Sahid Husain Secretary, Ministry of Water & Power, Government of Pakistan visited New Delhi during Jan 28 -Feb 1, '99 for the second round of discussions on the issue of exchange/export of power by Pakistan.

4

Rural Electrification Programme

Rural Electrification involves supply of energy for two types of programmes:

— Production oriented activities like minor irrigation rural industries etc., and

— Electrification of villages.

While the emphasis is laid on exploitation of ground water potential and energisation of pumpsets/tubewells, which has a bearing on agricultural production, the accent in respect of areas covered under the Revised Minimum Needs Programme (RMNP), is on village electrification.

The existing definition of village electrification was reviewed and changed in 1997. According to the earlier definition :

"A village is classified as electrified if electricity is being used within its revenue area for any purpose whatsoever."

This definition of village electrification was reviewed in consultation with the State Governments and State Electricity Boards and it was decided to adopt the following new definition:

"A village will be deemed to be electrified if electricity is used in the inhabited locality within the revenue boundary of the village for any purpose whatsover."

Ministry of power has circulated the new definition of Village Electrification to all State Governments/State Electricity Boards on 28th October, 1997 and advised them that the statistics of Village Electrification may be complied on the basis of new definition and reported to Central Electricity Authority.

During the year 1998-99, 236 inhabited villages were electrified and 96678 irrigation pumpsets/tubewells energised as on 30.11.1998. Cumulatively 502186 villages have been electrified and 11946084 pumpsets have been energised as on 30.11.1998.

As regards the electrification of tribal villages, out of a total of 115088 tribal villages in the country 81049 (provisional) villages constituting 70% have been electrified as on 30.11.1998. Similarly 291188 (provisional) Harijan Bastis have been electrified on the same date.

5

Energy Conservation, Renovation and Modernisation

Energy conservation

Conservation and efficient use of energy has been accorded high priority by the Government considering the need to bridge the gap between the demand and availability of various forms of commercial energy. Measures to conserve energy are being devised and implemented both on the supply side and the end use (demand) side. A budgetary provision of Rs. 6.00 crore (including Rs. 55 lakh for the Energy Management Centre) has been provided in 1997-98 for promoting energy conservation activities.

Supply side management

The measure adopted consists of studies for reduction of secondary fuel oil consumption in thermal power stations and detailed energy audit studies to identify measures for improving the efficiency of the generating stations.

Under Supply side Management measure, studies for reduction of fuel oil consumption at 6 Thermal Power Stations against the target of 6, Energy Audit tests at 4 thermal power stations against the target of 4 and combined Energy Audit Tests and studies for reduction of fuel oil consumption at 15 thermal power stations against the target of 23 were completed upto March'98. During the period April, '98-Nov. '98, Energy Audit tests were conducted at Obra & Dhuvarau TPSs and combined Energy Audit Tests and oil studies were carried out at I.P. Stn., Korba (E), Chandrapura (DVC, Tanda, Sikka & Patratu TPSs). Besides, preliminary visits to another 2 TPSs were also completed upto November '98. Reports in respect of studies for reduction of fuel oil consumption at 6 TPSs and Energy Audit reports in respect of 17 TPSs have been released upto Nov.'98. In view of the encouraging response from the TPSs and the results achieved consequent to implementation of the measures recommended in the Energy Audit Reports, a proposal for extension of the scheme to cover another 20 TPSs at an additional cost of Rs. 15 lakh has been prepared. The proposal is yet to be approved by MOP.

Based on the studies earlier carried out for reduction of secondary fuel oil consumption at Satpura, Parli, Titagarh, Durgapur (DVC), Bandel, and Bongaigaon Thermal Power Stations corrective steps were taken by the concerned power stations and there is a definite declining trend in secondary fuel oil consumption.

On All India level, there has been a continuous declining trend in Specific Secondary Fuel Oil Consumption at Thermal Power Stations. Against consumption of 6.77 ml/kwh during the year 1991-92, before beginning of the 8th plan, the corresponding figure during 1997-98 is 3.51 ml/kwh, resulting in a national saving of 9.81 lakh KL of FO costing about Rs. 690 crore during the year 1997-98 in comparison to 91-92 level.

Energy Audit Studies have revealed that the power stations were heavily losing due to poor condenser vacuum, non-availability of H.P. Heaters, excessive consumption of DM waters, air ingress into the boiler, high flue gas temperature etc. Studies carried out at Paricha, Khaperkheda and Sabarmati (AECO) Thermal

Power Stations revealed that each unit at these stations was incurring huge financial losses due to sub-optimal operations in terms of increased coal & oil consumption.

Based on guidelines issued for reduction in Transmission and Distribution losses and Energy Audit in Power System, utilities have been encouraged to reduce the T&D losses by implementing the schemes in regard to System Improvement, Energy Audit in Distribution System, Load Management and introduction of Time Of Use Tariffs (TOU) etc.

Demand side management

On the Demand side, Energy Conservation Schemes pertaining to various sectors - Agriculture, Industry, Domestic and Commercial were appraised to facilitate the release of grants/subsidies to the various agencies. Some of the schemes apprised/being implemented during 1997-98 are : Pilot projects for installation of Eurolights Energy saving lamps at various locations in MSEB, computerised Load Management Schemes at distribution level in MP, AP etc. Rectification of agricultural pumpsets in AP, installation of TOD Electronic meters in respect of Industrial Consumers in WBSEB, Energy Audit of Power Systems in HSEB, PSEB etc., Energy conservation in Aluminium Industries by employing titanium boride cathode, design & development of vector controlled induction motors in textile-industries, Schemes for cost sharing for Energy Efficient lightings in the States/UTs in IX plan etc.

An Environment Cell under the Conservation & Environment Division has been set up to serve as a focal point for the consideration of environmental related aspects of the power projects. The functions of the Cell inter-alia, include collection, collation of enviornmental related data for power projects, environmental upgradation of thermal projects, appraisal of EIA reports

& co-ordination with Ministry of Environment & Forests for cleanrace of power projects and related issues. An 'Expert Committee' reconstituted by Ministry of Environment and Forests in June, 1998 for environmental impact assessment of thermal power projects.

The reconstituted Expert Committee has considered 29 projects with an installed capacity of 15021.5 MW during June'98 to Nov. '98 of which 15 projects with an installed aggregate capacity of 7310 MW have been recommended for clearance from environmental angle.

Renovation and modernisation

In order to improve the performance of existing thermal Power Stations, a massive renovation and modernisation (R&M) Programme (Phase-I) was launched by the Government of India all over the country in Sept. '84 for completion during the Seventh Plan period. This programme has since been completed.

R&M (Phase-II) Programme

In view of the encouraging results achieved from the implementation of Phased of R&M programme, Phase-II programme for R&M of Thermal Power Stations was taken up in the year 1990-91 by the Government of India for implementation during the 8th Plan. Under this programme, 44 Nos. of Thermal Power Stations consisting of 198 Nos. Thermal Units aggregating to a total capacity of 20,869.435 MW are covered.

After the completion of the programme the benefits expected are : (i) additional generation of 7,864 MU/ Year (ii) increase of 100 MW peaking capacity (iii) life extension of 24 Nos. of Thermal Units by 15-20 years.

Progress

Physical : Out of a total of 1629 activities 787 activities have been completed. Out of the remaining, 245 Nos. are under progress. Life Extension works on 9 Nos. of units have been completed.

Financial : An amount of Rs. 1005 crore has been incurred till Nov., '98 with the financial assistance provided by PFC/World Bank as per details given

(Rs. in crores)

PFC	186.47
World Bank/OECF	210.47
State Plan Own Resources	607.73
Total Expenditure till Nov., '98	1004.67

Hydro Electric Power Stations

Based on the recommendations of the National Committee and subsequent reviews, a programme for renovation, modernisation and 'uprating of Hydro Power Stations was formulated by Central Electricity Authority in which 55 schemes where identified with an aggregate capacity of 9653 MW (210 Nos generating units). The total estimated cost of these schemes is Rs. 1493 Cr. and expected benefit is 2531 MW/7181 MU. Out of 55 schemes, work on 19 schemes at an estimated cost of Rs. 259. 4 Cr. and an expected benefit of 874 MW/ 1308 MU have been completed till 31.3.1998. During 1998-99, it was programmed to complete the following schemes:

	Scheme	Installed capacity (MW)	Estimated Cost (Rs.)	Expected Benefit MW/ MU	
1.	Bassi, H.P.	4×15	5.35	—/ 12.50	
2.	Hirakud	2×37.5	90.26	97.5	275
3.	Bhakra RB	5×120	77.5	185 /	310
4.	Kotla (UB)	2×24.2 + 1×29.25	18.90	27.63 /	249.48

Out of four above schemes, two schemes, viz. Hirakud (U1&2) and Kotla (U3) have been completed till 30.11.98. The RM&U scheme of Bassi H.E.P. is under advanced stage of implementation while the RM&U works at Bhakra RB (5x120MW) pertaining to Units 7 and 10 are held up due to non-despatch of stator punching being imported from Russia. 3 units out of 5 of Bhakra RB have been uprated from 120 MW to 157 MW.

In addition, 3 units of Koyana (I&II) (4x65MW + 4x75MW) and 1 unit of Hirakud II (3x24MW) have been recommissioned during 1998-99 after undergoing major RM&U works. At present there are 26 numbers of ongoing schemes where RM&U works at an estimated cost of Rs. 883 Crore and an expected benefit of 1233 MW/3954 MU are under different stages of implementation and are scheduled to be completed during the Ninth Plan. Remaining eight numbers of schemes with an estimated cost of Rs. 241 Crore and expected benefit of 299 MW/1399 MUs are awaiting financial tie-ups.

Further, new proposals have been sought from the State Authorities/Utilities for Hydro Power Stations/ Schemes that could be considered for RM&U work under Phase II. So far, 19 proposals have been received from the states.

6

Central Electricity Authority

Organisation of CEA

The Central Electricity Authority (CEA) is a statutory organisation constituted under Section 3(1) of the Electricity (Supply) Act, 1948. It was established as a part-time body in 1951 and made a full-time body in 1975. It is an attached office of Ministry of Power, Govt. of India.

In all technical, financial and economic matters, the Ministry of Power is assisted by the CEA. CEA is responsible for technical co-ordination and supervision of programmes and is also entrusted with a number of statutory functions. CEA is headed by a Chairman, who is also Ex-officio Secretary to the Government of India and has full-time Members, who are of the rank of Ex-officio Additional Secretaries to the Government of India.

Functions of CEA

The Authority is generally to exercise such functions and perform such duties and act in such a manner as the Central government may prescribe under the Rules framed under Section 413(1) of the Electricity (Supply) Act, 1948 or by issue of written directions in matters of policy involving public interest under Section 4A(l) of the said Act. Under Section 3(1) of the Act, the CEA is particularly charged with the following functions:

— To develop a sound, adequate and uniform national power policy, formulate short-term and perspective plans for power development and coordinate the activities of planning agencies in relation to the control and utilisation of national power resources;

— To collect and record the data concerning generation, distribution and utilisation of power and carry out studies relating to cost, efficiency, losses, benefits and such like matters;

— To make public from time to time information secured under the Act and to provide for the publication of reports and investigation;

— To advise any State Govt., SEB, Generating Company or any other agency engaged in generation or supply of electricity on such matters as will enable such Govt., SEB, generating company or agency to operate and maintain the power system under the ownership or control in an improved manner and where necessary in coordination with any other agency owning or having the control of another power system;

— To promote and assist in the timely completion of schemes sanctioned under Chapter V of the Act;

— To make arrangements for advancing the skill of persons in the generation and supply of electricity;

— To carry out or make arrangement for any investigation for the purpose of generating or transmitting electricity;

— To promote research in matters affecting the generation, transmission and supply of electricity;

— To advise the Central Govt. on any other matter on which its advice is sought or make recommendations to that Govt. on any matter if, in the opinion of the

Authority the recommendation would help in improving the generation, distribution and utilisation of electricity; and

— To discharge such other functions as may be entrusted to it or under any other law. Under the provision of Electricity (Supply) Act, 1948, the Central Govt. has further added a few more functions to the Central Electricity Authority. These are:

Co-ordination of research and development in the power generation field;

Evaluation of financial performance of the SEBs constituted under Section 5 and undertaking of studies concerning the economic and commercial aspects of the power industry as well as analysis of the tariff structure in the power industry;

Techno-economic appraisal of power projects; Promotion of inter-State and Joint Sector power projects.

Apart from the above functions provided under the Electricity (Supply) Act, CEA also undertakes design and engineering of power projects with a view to developing in-house technical know-how and also to assist the State Electricity Boards, Generating Companies & State authorities requiring such assistance under Section 3(1) (v) of the Electricity (Supply) Act, 1948.

Subordinate offices

Following are the subordinate offices of the CEA:

— Northern Regional Electricity Board, New Delhi
— Western Regional Electricity Board, Mumbai.
— Eastern Regional Electricity Board, Calcutta.
— Southern Regional Electricity Board, Bangalore.
— North-Eastern Regional Electricity Board, Shillong.
— Power System Training Institute, Bangalore.

— Hot Line Training Centre, Bangalore.
— Regional Power Survey Organisation at New Delhi.
— Regional Power Survey Organisation at Bangalore.
— Regional Power Survey Organisation at Mumbai
— Regional Power Survey Organisation at Calcutta.
— Regional Inspectorate Organisation at Chennai
— Regional Inspectorate Organisation at Goa.
— Regional Inspectorate Organisation at New Delhi.
— Regional Inspectorate Organisation at Shillong.

Techno-economic appraisal of power schemes

— During the year 1998-99 (upto 30.11.98), CEA accorded Techno-Economic Clearance to 27 Nos. of new power schemes comprising 20 generation schemes, 7 T&D schemes involving new capacity' addition of 7833 MW and 946 Ckt.Kms of transmission lines.

— During the year 1998-99 (upto 30.11.98), CEA consultation under Section 44 of E(S) Act, 1948 was issued to 6 Nos. captive power plants aggregating to 1106 MW to the various State electricity Boards.

The Thermal Civil Design Division of CGA provides necessary technical backup on Civil Engineering matters to other Wings/Divisions of CEA and Ministry of Power and other utilitites.

The detailed project report/revised cost estimates received in CEA for Techno economic clearance are perused in respect of civil works. The various inputs required for consideration of the scheme by the Standing Committee for Project Appraisal (SPAC) are first checked and the SPAC meeting convened. Additional clarifications required are obtained during SPAC. The scheme is finally approved in the meeting.

The transmission schemes are also appraised and TEC accorded.

Monitoring of fly ASH utilisation

TCD has carried out the monitoring of utilisation of flyash that is being produced in various coal based thermal power stations in the country. The data in regard to flyash generation and utilisation for the year 1997-98 received from 28 Nos. of coal based thermal power stations was examined and compiled.

Design and consultancy

Thermal Civil Designs Division has provided engineering services for the following ongoing thermal power projects and transmission schemes of various power utilities

— Ash handling system, DM Plant and Cooling Tower of Faridabad TPS (Haryana) (3x60MW)

— 400 KV Transmission System of APSEB for evacuating Power from Srisailam HEP. This consists of 400 KV Transmission lines and 2 nos. of 400/220 KV substations, one at Hyderabad and the other at Kurnool.

— Retrofitting of ESP Units I & II of Panipat TPS (2x110MW) Haryana.

— Rehabilitation of 220 KV D/C transmission line for Ganga River crossing near Patna of Bihar State Electricity Board.

— Augmentation of ash handling system of existing Unit I to V of DVB.

— Consultancy for the proposed Gas based Pragati Power Project 360 MW of DVB proposed

— Transmission Line Tower foundations for Tala HEP, Bhutan (proposed).

Power development in national capital region

CEA has undertaken detailed techno-economic feasibility studies for the towns of Manesar in Haryana, Bhiwadi in

Rajasthan and Ghaziabad in UP relating to setting up of captive power generation plants including transmission and distribution network for these towns corresponding to 2007 AD. Assessment of additional requirement of generation, transmission and model distribution facilities will be done after demand forecasting.

Assistance to the UTs

CEA is responsible for power development in the UTs. As such, it renders assistance to the UTs in Project formulation and preparation of specification/ procurement of equipments pertaining to power generation/transmission and distribution schemes. The assistance rendered to various UT's during the year 1998-99 is as given below:

Technical Assistance/Appraisal of Schemes in A&N Islands

— (i) A technical team by Shri M.K.Garg, Director (LIT) visited the Andaman and Nicobar islands to take stock of the power crisis and to suggest remedial measures.

— Interim scheme for augmentation of DG capacity at Rangat Bay by 1x1000 KVA DG set at a cost of Rs. 1.62 crores.

Lakshadweep

Scheme for augmentation of Diesel Generating capacity and distribution system at Minicoy Island during the Ninth Five Year Plan.

Monitoring of thermal projects

In order to keep a close watch for timely completion of sanctioned and on-going- thermal power projects in the Central, State and Private Sector, implementation of the projects is closely monitored by Thermal Monitoring Division in Thermal Wing, CEA. Project-wise bottlenecks are identified, remedial measures are suggested and concerned project authorities are advised to undertake requisite steps/actions to overcome the constraints. Joint Coordination Meetings are held twice a year and review meetings held periodically which provide useful link between project authorities and main suppliers of equipment to ensure coordinated efforts for timely completion of thermal projects under execution.

Design and engineering consultancy of transmission system

Design and engineering consultancy services are being rendered by CEA for following transmission systems:

— 400 KV transmission lines and substations associated with 900 MW Srisailam Left Bank Power House Transmission System of APSEB.

— 400 KV transmission lines & substations associated with 1020 MW Tala HEP of Bhutan.

Functions of energy policy division

— Coordination of long term linkage for coal, oil and gas.

— Energy Pricing for different fuels for power generation.

— Energy and Power Policy.

— Coordination of R&D activities in power sector.

Committee on hydro tariff

In pursuance of the decision taken in the meeting by Principal Secretary to the Prime Minister on 25.9.1996, a Committee was set up in CEA for formulation of hydro tariff with a view to attracting private investment in hydro power development. Subsequently, based on the directives of National Task Force (NTF), the Committee was enlarged to include representatives from other organisations like NHPC, TNEB, KPCL, NEEPCO, BBMB & POWERGRID. The Committee submitted its report in

August, 1998. In view of the Hydro Policy announced by Government of India in August, 1998, NTF directed the committee to review its recommendations in the light of it's provisions.

Review of targets/ achievements during the year 98-99

A programme of commissioning of 2754.8 MW additional thermal generating capacity was envisaged at the beginning of the year 1998-99 As per the latest status some of the thermal units are likely to be preponed and get commissioned within the year 1998-99. The total thermal capacity addition now expected to be achieved during 1998-99 is 3834.1 MW as explained below:

— Thermal capacity already commissioned during the year 1998-99 till the end of January, 1999 (Details are at statement) : 1364.20 MW

— Thermal capacity likely to be commissioned during the balance period of 1998-99 (Details are at statement): 2469.9 MW

7

Private Sector Participation

The Indian Electricity Scenario

Since independence, development of the electricity sector has primarily been the responsibility of the Government, with a relatively small contribution from private enterprises, in the form of licensees like Bombay Suburban Electricity Supply Company (BSES), Tata Electricity Company JEC), Calcutta Electric Supply Company (CESC) and Ahmedabad Electric Company (AEC), etc. However, considering the large requirement of funds for the sector, it is not possible to mobilise adequate financial resources by Government alone, given the highly capital intensive nature of the sector and the large incremental capacity addition requirements. At present, the country faces an energy shortage of about 8.3% and peaking shortage of around 11.3%. The situation is likely to worsen due to the anticipated slippage in the planned capacity addition.

Against this background, and to mobilise additional resources for the sector to help bridge the gap in demand and supply, the Government formulated a policy in 1991 with the objective to encourage greater investment by private enterprises in the electricity sector. The Electricity (Supply) Act, 1948 was amended in 1991 to provide a legal framework for facilitating the investments. Although the policy announced in 1991 covers generation an distribution, there has been more progress in the area of generation in so far as private sector is concerned.

The package of incentives in the policy which complements the amended provision in the legislation comprehensively cover the legal, administrative and financial environment to make investments in the sector attractive. A two-part tariff system for power projects to be put up by the Independent Power Producers covering the fixed costs and variable energy cost in electricity pricing, has been formulated and tariff notification issued in March 1992. This notification inter-alia, provides for a 16% Return Equity at 68.5% PLF for thermal plants (coal/lignite/gas) and 90% availability for hydro electric plants. An amendment to the tariff notification issued on 23.5.1997 lays down the norms for thermal generating stations awarded through a process of competitive bidding. To encourage efficiency in plant operation, an incentive scheme based on capacity utilisation has also been formulated.

Response from the private sector

Private power projects being monitored by Central Government: The response to GOI's energy policy has been encouraging. Since 1991, both domestic and foreign developers have evinced keen interest in the Indian power sector. Altogether, 92 private power projects are presently being monitored by the Central Government, amounting to 50,868 MW of installed generation capacity. In addition, there are several projects which are being set up by the private sector with the approval of the State Governments themselves and do not require the techno-economic clearance of CEA.

Projects tech no-economically cleared by CEA: So far, 49 private sector power projects amounting to around 23.137 MW have been given techno-economic clearance by Central Electricity Authority (CEA).

Projects commissioned/under construction: Around 17 private sector power generation projects having a total capacity of about 3018 MW have so far been commissioned. This includes projects set up by licensee companies etc., which do not require the concurrence of the CEA. Apart from this, 18 projects with a total capacity of around 4241MW are under construction out of which 2 projects for 317.5 MW have been partially commissioned.

Major policy initiatives taken to streamline the process of project development

Model Power Purchase Agreement: Model PPAs for thermal power projects and hydro-electric power projects prepared by international consultants have been circulated.

Competitive bidding for Awarding Projects: The initial batch of projects were awarded generally on the basis of negotiations between the SEB and single developer. The SEBs and State Governments were advised to introduce a more competitive element in the process of selection of developers and award of projects, and consider awarding new projects only on the basis of competitive bidding. In January '95, it was decided that no new private power project proposal would be considered by CEA, if the project is not awarded through competitive bidding. A cut off date 18.2.95 was to have been treated as valid. Projects after this date have to be awarded only after following the competitive bidding route. However, certain categories of projects, where the ICB route may not be feasible, have been exempted from this route. Detailed guidelines have also been issued to the State Governments for adopting competitive bidding.

Exemption from ICB route:

It has been recognised that in order to have the benefit of the already existing infrastructure facilities, which results in reduced project costs, it would be preferable for the same project developer to be allowed to undertake the expansion project rather than to undergo the bidding process for selecting a new developer. The states have accordingly been advised in January, 1997 to encourage such expansion plants by IPPs.

Joint venture projects between SEB/PSU and private company

Competitive bidding shall not be necessary for selection of the private company partner in such joint venture projects where the SEB/Public Sector Undertaking holds majority shares of the joint venture company.

Generating stations exclusively for captive use

Competitive bidding would not be required for setting up generating stations by IPP exclusively for the captive use of an industry or a group of industries without involving any sale to State Grid.

Bidding for EPC contracts

The States/SEBs had been advised in June 1996 to impress upon the promoters that for the projects that have not finalised their EPC contracts, it would be necessary to follow the ICB route in the selection of their EPC contractors. In the case of IPPs who inform that their EPC contracts have been finalised, the SEB should satisfy itself that they have actually done so and in cases where it is not finalised, the SEB should ensure that the bidding route adopted is transparent and proper.

Guidelines for private sector participation in renovation and modernisation

The policy details out various options like lease, rehabiliate, operate and transfer (LROT), sale of plant and Joint Venture between SEBs and private companies for promoting R&M programmes. While deciding on the availiable options, the policy emphasizes on adherence to competitive bidding route. R&M schemes costing up to Rs. 500 crore are not required to be submitted to the CEA for appraisal.

Captive/Co-generation Plants: As an alternative to meet the rapidly increasing industrial demand for power, Ministry of Power has suggested encouragement to captive/co-generation plants by industries. The policy suggests, inter-alia, sale of excess power to the grid as per mutually agreed rates, access to transmissions grid of the State on payment of wheeling charges, third party access for direct sale of power etc. A resolution for promotion of co-generation has also been issued on November 6, 1996. The resolution details the definition of co-generation, mode of fixation of tariff and mode of deciding co-generation status for the power plants.

Liquid Fuel Policy: Even though the response of the private sector to set up coal/lignite, gas and hydroelectric projects was encouraging, it was recognised that in view of the long gestation period these projects would take three to five years to come on stream. Hence, a quick capacity addition was essential in order to avert a severe power crisis. After detailed examination of the matter in consultation with Ministry of Petroleum and Natural Gas and Planning Commission, and a detailed study through computer modelling, it was felt that there was economic wisdom in setting up liquid fuel based power plants in certain areas of the country, which have a comparatively shorter period of gestation. Accordingly, It was decided to permit setting up of power projects based on heavy fuel oils such as, Naphtha, Heavy Petroleum Stock (HPS), Low Sulphur Heavy Stock (LSHS), Heavy Furnace Oil (HFO), Furnace Oil (FO) Vaccume Residue Petroleum Coke and Natural Gas, wherever available, as primary fuel.

Considering the constraints with liquid fuels for

power generation, it was decided in 1996 that liquid fuel based power projects corresponding to a total generation capacity of around 12,000 MW could be put up.

Recent modifications in the Liquid Fuel Policy: The last date for achieving financial closure for liquid fuel based power projects for which linkages have already been issued was 31.3.98.

A number of requests were received to extend this date, give additional linkages for new projects and for putting up power projects based on non-traditional fuels like condensate & orimulsion. All these requests were examined and the following decisions were taken in July, 1998.

— The existing ceiling of 12000 MW allocated to various States would apply only to naphtha. This would be in addition to the FO/LSHS linkages already given.

— States would thus, be free to contract for new power projects based on FO beyond the existing linkages. Taking in to account the environmental implications it will be mandatory for such new FO based power plants, beyond the existing linkages to use Integrated Gasification combined Cycle (IGGC) technology, or any other technology that would bring sulphur content to within acceptable limits.

— Already, LSHS is on OGL and this freedom would be extended for non-traditional fuels like condensate and orimulsion subject to actual user condition.

— There would be no obligation for Oil PSUs to give fresh linkages for any new projects, except naphtha based projects within a ceiling of 12000MW and projects based on other fuels for which linkages have already been issued.

— HSD would be permitted for power generation only

as a special case in inaccessible and isolated areas where small diesel based capacities are sought to be set up and where use of other fuels is not feasible.

— For all the existing projects, the last date for financial closure would be 31st October, 1998. However, since the majority of projects were not able to achieve financial closure, the deadline was again extended upto 31.1.1999.

Setting up of Mega Power Projects: The guidelines for setting up of mega power projects were initially issued in November, 1995. Accordingly, power projects having a capacity of 1000 MW or above and supplying power to more than one State were defined as a mega power project. After considering the experience of this policy, the policy has been revised in November, 1998. As per the new policy, Inter-state and Inter-regional mega power projects are proposed to be set up both in the public and private sectors.

The Standing Independent Group (SIG) which had been constituted by the Government of India in November, 1997, to establish parameters for negotiation of large power generation projects would initially be the apex body to oversee the implementation of the mega private power projects. The principles of competitive bidding would be adhered to as far as possible, while obtaining tariff offers.

A Power Trading Company (PTC) would be established. Security to the PTC would be provided by means of a Letter of Credit and recourse to the Sate's share of Central Plan allocations and other devolutions. A precondition would be that the beneficiary States should have constituted their Regulatory Commissions with full powers to fix tariffs as envisaged in the Central Act and have privatised the distribution of power in cities having population of more than one million.

The import of capital equipment would be free of customs duty for these projects In order to ensure that domestic bidders are not adversely affected price preference of 15% would be given for the projects under Public Sector, while deemed export benefits as per the EXIM policy would be given to Domestic Bidders for projects both under Public and Private Sector.

The domestic bidders would be allowed to quote in US Dollars or any other foreign currency of their choice. In addition, the income-tax holiday regime would be continued with the provision that the tax holiday period of 10 years can be claimed by a promoter in any block of 10 years, within the first 15 years. The State Governments are requested to exempt supplies made to megapower plants from sales tax and local levies.

It is visualised that the country would be adding 15,000 - 20,000 MW of capacity through this policy at the most competitive tariffs payable by State Electricity Boards and consequently by consumers.

Enhancing the CEA limit: A notification was issued in December, 1995 enhancing the limit of capital expenditure of the schemes requiring concurrence of CEA from Rs. 100 crore to Rs 400 crore in case of generating station schemes put up by a Generating Company selected through a process of competitive bidding by the competent Government. The limit was further enhanced to Rs. 1000 crore in September, 1996.

The limit in respect of different categories of power schemes beyond which the concurrence of CEA would be required, has been further changed in November 1998 as follows:

— in relation to a scheme for thermal generating station prepared by a Generating Company selected through a process of competitive bidding by the competent

Government or Governments and conforming to the factors notified vide number S.O. 251(E), dated the 30th March, 1992 as amended vide number S.O. 410(E), dated the 23rd May, 1997, Rupees Five Thousand Crore;

— in relation to a schemes for other thermal generating station prepared by a Generating Company selected through a process of competitive bidding by the competent Government or Governments, Rupees One Thousand Crore;

— in relation to a scheme for hydro-electric generating station prepared by a Generating Company selected through a process of competitive bidding by the competent Government or Governments, Rupees One Thousand Crore;

— in relation to a scheme for renovation and modernisation of existing power generating stations, Rupees Five Hundred Crore; and

— in relation to all other schemes, Rupees Two Hundred and Fifty Crore;

Policy on Automatic Approval for Foreign Direct Investment : Vide a press note issued in January, 1997, by the Ministry of Industry, it was decided to allow automatic approval for foreign equity upto 74% in certain areas of the power sector.

The Government has recently reviewed the existing guidelines on automatic approval for foreign equity for electric generation, transmission and distribution projects, and has decided to enlarge the provisions for automatic approval for such projects.

Accordingly, projects for electric generation, transmission and distribution will be permitted foreign equity participation up to 100% on the automatic approval route provided the foreign equity in any such project does not exceed Rs. 1500 crore. The categories which would qualify for such automatic approval are:

- Hydro-electric power plants
- Coal/lignite based thermal power plants
- Oil/gas based thermal power plants

New norms for environmental clearance: The following delegations have been made to the Stàte Governments in the matter of environment clearance to power projects:

- All co-generation plants and captive power plants upto 250 MW
- Coal based plants upto 500 MW using fluidised bed technology subject to sensitive area restrictions.
- Power stations upto 250 MW on conventional technology.
- Gas/Naphtha based station upto 500 MW-

A new procedure for getting environmental clearance for pithead thermal project has also been laid down.

Relaxation of 40% capital for debt exposure by IFIs:
The policy announced in 1991 envisaged that, an amount not exceeding 40% of the total outlay for private sector units may come from Indian Public Financial Institutions (IPFIs).

The Government has now decided that while there will be no bar to the extent of domestic debt raised by a project developer, subject to the need of maximising financing from external sources and prudential norms exercised by IPFIs, allowing a higher domestic debt component for projects which are developed based on indigenously sourced plant and equipment, would be more desirable.

It has also been decided that there would be no objection for Foreign Term Loan being replaced by Rupee Term Loan as long as the hard cost does not change and the new financial arrangements are acceptable to the concerned SEB/State Government, project developers and the lenders. Whenever such a change is desired in the financial package, project developers may approach CEA, for formal approval.

8

Cooperation with Neighbouring Countries in Hydro Power

Development of water resources of the common rivers of India neighbouring countries of Nepal and Bhutan for mutual benefits has been under discussions with these countries. There is regular exchange of electric power between India and the above neighbouring countries for the supply of surplus power and meeting power requirements in the border areas.

India has been assisting Nepal in the utilisation of its hydro power potential and four HE schemes viz. Pokhara, Trisuli, Western Gandak and Devighat have been implemented with financial and technical assistance from Govt. of India. Three major water resources projects in Nepal viz. Karnali, Pancheshwar and Saptakoshi are presently under discussions at various levels as mutual benefit projects. Feasibility report of Karnali multipurpose project (1080 MW) was prepared in 1989. Key parameters of this project are to be finalised after mutual discussions. Investigations have been carried out in respect of Pancheshwar MPP by the two countries in their respective territories. Additional investigations and studies required to be carried out have jointly been listed. Preparation of joint DPR is presently under discussions. Development of this project is covered under integrated Mahakali River Treaty signed between HMG, Nepal and India in February, 1996 and subsequently ratified. India had offered financial and technical assistance for investigation of saptakoshi (3300 MW) Multi-purpose project. Joint technical experts groups have been constituted for each of the above projects for joint guidance for carrying out investigations and preparation of detailed project reports (DPRs).

In Bhutan, Chukha H.E. Project (336 MW) implemented with Indian financial and technical assistance and operating in an excellent manner is a shining example of cooperation between the two countries for mutual benefits. Surplus power from the project, is being imported by India. Kurichu H.E. project (45 MW) in Eastern Bhutan is presently under implementation on a turnkey basis with Indian financial and technical assistance. Another project viz. Tala H.E. Project (1020 MW), has been taken up for implementation and is being executed by Tala Hydro-electric Project Authority (THPA) comprising of Indian and Bhutanese Officers and Engineers. Consultancy for the project in respect of both electro-mechanical and Civil works is being rendered by Central Electricity Authority (CEA), Central Water Commission (CWC) and Water & Power Consultancy Services (WAPCOS). The project is being funded by India through grant and loan and major portion of the power generated will be made available to India. Investigations of Sankosh Multi-purpose Project (4060 MW) have been completed by CWC and DPR prepared by CEA/CWC.

Investigations of two Hydro-electric projects namely Wangchu (900 MW) and Bunakha (180 MW) have been completed and DPR prepared. India is also providing technical assistance for rehabilitation of 8 Nos. Mini/ Micro hydel projects in Bhutan for which CEA is rendering Design and Engineering Consultancy Services.

9

Badarpur Thermal Power Station

Performance

Badapur Thermal Power Station consists of 3x100 MW and 2x210 MW coal fired units with an installed capacity of 720 MW. However, the 3 units of 100 MW each have been derated to 95MW w.e.f. 11.1.1990. The station is owned by Government of India and is being managed by NTPC since 1st April 1978. Presently the entire energy generated at this station is supplied to the Delhi Vidyut Board only.

The generation target for BTPS has been fixed at 4300 MUs at a PLF of 69.63% for the year 1998-99. Till Nov.'98, the station has already generated 3087.63 MUs at a PLF of 74.8%.

Renovation & modernisation

Phase-I

BTPS is one of the Thermal Power Station identified under the centrally sponsored scheme for Renovation and Modernisation of thermal utilities. Under the Renovation & Modernisation Scheme, Phase-I, various schemes for 3x100 MW of BTPS for Rs. 36.97 crore had been approved.

Most of the schemes have already been implemented and an expenditure of Rs.35.54 crore has been incurred upto 30th November 1998. With implementation of

R&M-1 scheme for BTPS the actual annual average PLIF has improved from 45.30% to 65.00% against the estimated improvement in PLF from 45.30% to 55.00%. The result of successful R&M programme of BTPS has turned out to be exemplary. During the calender year 1998 the station generated. 4710 MUs, the highest since inception.

Phase-II

Under R&M Phase-if programme, certain areas were identified for carrying out further modification. BTPS submitted a proposal for R&M Phase-II for an estimated cost of Rs. 187.77 crores for approval covering all units of BTPS.

The proposal has been techno-economically cleared by CEA and approved by PIB in April 1997. At present, the proposal is under process for approval by CCEA. The scheme mainly emphasises on reduction in heat rate increase in PLIF from 65.00% to 70.00% and increase in generation by about 320 MUs/year.

Urgent works of capital nature

Pending execution of R&M Phse-II certain urgent works of capital nature were identified jointly with CEA for immediate implementation in the BTPS units. These schemes have been approved by Ministry of Power for execution during the year 1998-99 & 1999-2000, at an estimated cost of Rs. 14.70 crore. After execution of these works there will be improvement in safety, reliability and availability of the units and also reduction in maintenance cost.

Ash utilisation

Ash utilisation for 1998-99 has been targeted as 30% out of which 25% has already been achieved upto Nov.1998.

Production of ash bricks is also gaining momentum.

Out of the targeted 60 lakh bricks BTPS has already achieved a progress of 30 lakh bricks till Nov. 1998. IIT, Delhi, US Embassy and CBRI, Roorkee has taken approx. 2 lakh bricks for their construction works. Another area of ash utilisation is filling upto lowlying areas. CPWD for their CAG (Comptroller and Auditor General of India) Building Project in NOIDA (U.P.) has taken 30,000 cubic meters of fly ash for this purpose.

10

Public Sector Undertakings and Other Organisations

National thermal power corporation (NTPC)

National Thermal Power Corporation Ltd. (NTPC) was set up in 1975, as a central sector generating company for the development of thermal power. The corporation is at present engaged in operating/setting up of several Thermal Power Projects and Gas based power projects. The total approved investment of the corporation as on 30.11.98 stands at Rs. 36519.48 crore (excluding the investment on Transmission Systems which have since been transferred to Power Grid). Govt. of India has identified NTPC as one of the Navratnas —a potential 'Global Giant'. NTPC is a schedule 'A' organisation.

The approved capacity of NTPC Projects is 20515 MW. The capacity commissioned upto 30.11.98 is 16910 W This includes acquisition of Unchahar (420 MW) from UPRVUN in Feb.'92 and Talcher (460 MW) from Orissa SEB in June'95 and test synchronising of 115 MW Gas Turbine Generator Unit-1 of Kayamkulam CCPP. Presently, NTPC has to its credit 12 coal based thermal power projects and 7 gas/liquid fuel based combined cycle project.

Besides its own stations, NTPC also manages the Badarpur Thermal Power Station in Delhi Balco's Power Station near Korba, Madhya Pradesh (270 MW), which was also constructed by NTPC.

NTPC performance highlights: 1998-99 (As on 30.11.1998)

- A record generation; of over 69581.5 Million Units was achieved, as against the same period last years generation of 68246.3 Million Units.
- Techno-economic clearance accorded for Kawas-II, Anta-II, Auraiya-II and Gandhar-II.
- 115 MW GT-1 of Kayamkulam CCPP test synchronised on 2.11.98, 5 months ahead of schedule.
- Setting up of a Joint Venture Company with ABB proposed for Renovation and Modernisation.
- A loan of DM 53.98 million has been prepaid through fresh borrowing at cheaper rate of interest resulting savings in interest cost of Rs.2.70 crore during the balance life of loan.
- First time in the country, a Super Thermal Power Station (Korba) gets ISO-9002 certification.
- MOU signed with ONGC for setting up power plants under Joint Ventures based on residual fuel.
- Some projects have been identified for capacity addition by NTPC under Mega Projects Policy of Government of India. These are: Kahalgaon-II (1500 MW), North Karanpura (2000 MW), Barh (2000 MW), Cheyyur (1500 MW) and 1300 MW each at Anta, Auraiya, Kawas and Gandhar.
- Consultancy Wing received 9 orders. Total value of orders received during the period is Rs.817.875 Lac. This includes two major orders, one of Rs. 270 Lac from PGCIL, and another of Rs. 450 Lac from GIPC.
- Billing during 1998-99, upto 30.11.98, was Rs. 8937.79 crore with realisation of Rs 7677.19 crore i.e. 85.9%.

Generation

As on 30.11.98 a total capacity of 16795 MW (including Talcher TPS-460 MW) was under commercial operation at various NTPC stations. This comprises 30 Units of 200/210 MW at Singrauli, Korba, Ramagundam, Farakka, Vindhyachal, Dadri, Unchahar and Kahalgaon, 14 units of 500 MW at Singrauli, Korba, Ramagundam, Rihand, Farakka and Talcher and 26 gas/steam turbine units of various capacities operating at gas based combined cycle plants at Anta, Auraiya, Kawas, Dadri and Jhanor Gandhar gas based power projects.

The generation performance of NTPC Stations has consistently been at high level. Against the target of 104000 MUs (MOU excellent target for the year 199899), the gross generation from NTPC stations has been 69581.5 MUs, upto 30.11.98. During the year 1998-99, upto 30.11.98, the coal based units under commercial operation generated 56973.7 MUs as compared to 56417.3 MUs last year for the same period.

The PLF of coal based stations excluding stations of eastern region during this period (1998-99) was 82.3% against 81.7% last year for the same period. However, including Eastern Region, the PLF is only 72.2% due to low PLF in Eastern Region which results due to poor power demand and inadequate inter-regional transmission network.

Stations Managed by NTPC

Badarpur Thermal Power Station (BTPS) (705 MW) owned by Government of India is being managed by NTPC since 1st April, 1978. 100% power from this station is supplied to DVB. During the year 1998-99, upto 30.11.98, the station has generated 3087.6 MUs at a PLF of 74.8%, as against 2880.0 MUs at a PLF of 69.8% during the same period last year.

Balco Captive Power Plant (4x67.5 MW)

During the year 1998-99, upto 30.11.98, BCPP has generated 1310.9 Mus at a PLF of 82.9%.

World bank loan for NTPC power generation projects

During the year 1998-99, for the period April, 1998 to November 1998, NTPC has utilised US$ 130.53 million (Rs.568.03 cr.) out of the first tranche of time slice loan of US$ 400 million extended by World Bank to support NTPC's investment programme for Vindhyachal Stage-II, Kayamkulam and EAP for certain operating stations. The cumulative utilisation till 30.11.98 is US$ 393.10 million (Rs. 1533.36 cr.).

ADB loan for feroze Gandhi TPS stage-II (2x210 MW)

The ADB have approved NTPC as the implementing agency for stage-II of Feroze Gandhi Unchahar Thermal Power Project under loan for US$ 145 million consequent to take over of the project by NTPC. The transfer of the loan has been made effective from 14.11.1995 and an amount of US$ 15.42 million (Rs.64.76 crore) has been utilised in the financial year 1998-99, during the period April'98 to November'98. The cumulative utilisation till 30.11.98 is US$ 106.94 million (Rs.400.98 crores).

OECF assistance for Faridabad GPP (400 MW)

Faridabad Combined Cycle Gas based Power Project (400 MW) is being implemented with financial assistance from OECF, Japan. OECF has extended financial assistance of Japanese Yen 23.536 billion for the project. As per the revised allocation made by OECF, Japanese Yen 23.192 billion shall be available to NTPC for implementation of the project and the balance would be available for implementation of ATS by POWERGRID. The Govt. of India conveyed investment approval in July, 1997. The implementation of the project has taken off. Main plant turnkey package was awarded in Jan.'98. During the year 1998-99, upto 30.11.98, NTPC has utilised Japanese Yen 655.80 million (Rs.19.67crore). The cumulative utilisation till 30.11.98 is Japanese Yen 3625.80 million (Rs. 108.78 crore).

OECF Assistance for simhardi TPP (1000 MW)

Simhadri TPP (1000 MW) was posed to OECF, Japan for funding who have pledged a direct OECF loan of Japanese Yen 19,817 million to NTPC as first tranche loan for Simhadri TPP. The loan agreement has also been signed and the loan has become effective from 24.6.97. Investment approval for the project was given in July 1997. Main plant order for Simhadri has been placed on M/s BHEL, in November, 1998.

Memorandum of understanding

NTPC is the first power sector corporation to have signed a Memorandum of Understanding (MOU) with the Govt. of India and has been rated "Excellent" for the eleventh consecutive year (every year since inception of MOU system of rating).

In respect of major performance parameters, the MOU targets are given below:

Sl.No	Target 1998-99 V. good	Excellent
1. Generation (MUs)	99000	104000
2. Heat Rate (Kcal/Kwh)	2480	2470
3. Gross Margin (Rs. Cr.)	4460.01	4645.25
4. Net Profit to Capital employed%	6.85%	7.56%
5. Ash Utilisation (Lakh M^3)	21	23

Outstanding dues of NTPC

The billing for the year 1998-99 (upto 30.11.98) stood at Rs.9305.43 crore with realisation of Rs. 7879.89 crore, i.e. 84.7%. The total outstanding dues rose to Rs.9111.96 crore as on 30.11.98. The outstandings in terms of billing month works out to 5.8. There has been a significant improvement in the UC opened as on 30.11.98 being Rs.1037.63 crore, as against Rs.997.40 crore as on

31.3.1998. Currently, the UC covers 103.69% of the average monthly billing.

Growth strategy

NTPC is making significant contribution for the growth of the economy by generating more than one-fourth of India's total power generation with less than one-fifth capacity.

NTPC continued its multipronged strategy for capacity addition to maintain/augment its share in the country's installed generating capacity through green field projects, expansion of its existing plants, acquisition of SEBs plants and forming Joint Ventures and selective diversification in related areas.

VIII Plan

During VIII Plan period (1992-97) NTPC added 5462 MW including 460 MW of Talcher TPS taken over from Orissa SEB. Capacity addition done by NTPC accounts for more than 30% of country's capacity addition in VIII Plan period.

IX Plan

NTPC is planning to add a total of 5800 MW (3200 MW from ongoing projects and 2600 MW from New Projects) in the IX Plan. Out of 3200 MW of ongoing projects, NTPC has already added 115 MW during the IX Plan, by test synchronising 115 MW GT-I of Kayamkulam CCPP, 5 months ahead of schedule. The details of the projects are as follows:

Ongoing project

The following projects, for which investment approval has already been accorded, have been taken up for implementation and are scheduled to be commissioned in the IX Plan period:

Project (Location)	Capacity (Mw)	Capacity Addition in IX Plan (MW)	Commissioning Schedule
Vindhyachal-II (Madhya Pradesh)	1000	1000	Feb.2001
Unchahar-II (Uttar Pradesh)	420	420	Jul.'2000
Kayamkulam (Kerala)	350	350	Mar.'2000
Faridabad (Haryana)	430	430	Jan.'2000
Simhadri (Andhra Pradesh)	1000	1000	Mar.'2002
Total	3200	3200	

In addition, the following expansion projects have been envisaged for commissioning in the IX Plan:

Project	Location (MW)	Total Capacity in IX Plan (MW)	Capacity Addition
Kawas-II	Gujarat	650	650
Anta-II	Rajasthan	650	650
Auraiya-II	Uttar Pradesh	650	650
Gandhar-II	Gujarat	650	650
Total	2600	2600	

Beyond IX plan NTPC is planning to become a "33000 MW plus" company by the year 2007. The following projects have been identified for capacity addition beyond IX Plan:

Project	State	Capacity (MW)
1 .Talcher II	Orissa	2000
2. Sipat	MID	2000
3. Rihand II	UP	1000

4. Ramagundam III	AP	500
5. South Chennai (Cheyuur)	Tamil Nadu	1000
6. Kawas III	Gujarat	650
7. Gandhar III	Gujarat	650
8. Kahalgaon II	Bihar	1500
9. Kayamkulam II	Kerala	1950
10. North Karanpura	Bihar	2000
11. Barh	Bihar	2000

Joint ventures

UPL has been incorporated for Construction, Erection and Project Management work in Power Sector and other sectors in India and abroad. UPL has raised the authorised share capital from Rs.50 lakh to Rs.2 crore and additional equity of Rs. 93.10 lakh has been subscribed by NTPC. UPL is executing various orders including R&M of a power plant in Bangladesh.

HYDRO power and wind power

TPC initiated action for identification of Hydro projects. TPC is making detailed assessment of some selected projects in the upper reaches of Uttar Pradesh. Projects in other states are also being explored. The company has short-listed three sites for wind power project in Tamil nadu and Kerala. A consultant has been appointed for preparation of FR/DPR for selection of the best site for the first wind farm having a capacity of 20 MW.

Renovation and modernisation

Renovation and Modernisation (R&M) of old and under performing power stations of SEBs have been identified as a thrust area for quick and cost effective route for bridging growing gap between availability and demand of power in India. Keeping this in view, National Thermal Power Corporation Limited has decided to enter into a Joint Venture (JV) with ABB, Kraftwerke AG, Germany for R&M of power plants in India and abroad. NTPC has started discussions with ABB for finalisation and signing of MOU.

National Hydroelectric Power Corporation (NHPC)

National Hydroelectric Power Corporation Ltd. (NHPC) was incorporated in 1975 under Companies Act, 1956. The mission of NHPC is to harness the vast hydro, tidal and wind potential of the country to produce cheap/ pollution-free and inexhaustible power.

NHPC would play a significant role in the integrated and efficient development of hydroelectric, tidal and wind power in the Central Sector covering all aspects such as investigation, planning, designs, construction, operation and maintenance of hydroelectric, tidal and wind power projects. NHPC is a schedule 'A' Enterprise of the Government of India with an Authorised Share Capital of Rs.5,000 crores. With an investment base of over Rs.10,000 crore, NHPC is among the TOP TEN companies in the country in terms of investment.

Status of operating power stations

NHPC power stations generated 8228.7 MUs (upto November, 1998) against the target of 7062 MUs i.e. 1166.7 MUs (16.5%) more than the target. It was also higher by 1609 MUs (22.8%) than the generation of corresponding period of previous year. This has been achieved by adopting modern management techniques and better R&M of operating projects; which has resulted in increased energy generation during the last few years.

Status of ongoing projects:

Rangilt H.E. Project (60 MW): Concreting of 36,295 cum. (i.e.50.4%) has been completed in dam, against the total requirement of 72,000 cum. Head Race Tunnel has been daylighted and the Overt Lining thereof is in progress. Erection of Draft Tube, Scroll Casing and Upper Pit Liner Stator cores and Core flux testing have been completed in respect of all the 3 Generating Units. Rotor building and Stator windings of the Unit-3 have been completed. 132/ 66 kV Switchyard is ready in all respects. It has been back charged on 26.11.98. The project is scheduled for completion by March-June, 1999.

Dulhasti H.E. Project (390 MW): In Head Race Tunnel excavation of 4.4.884 Kms (i.e.46%) has been achieved out of the total length of 10.6 Kms. Out of the total requirement of 2,15,638 cum. concreting, 1, 18,916 cum. (i.e.55%) has been achieved in the Concrete Dam. 100% of the Excavation has been achieved in regard to the Switchyard, Transformer cavern, Pressure shaft and Upper expansion gallery.

In the Power House cavern 77% and in the Transformer cavern 88% of the total Concreting has been completed. In Unit-3, erection of Upper and Lower pit liners have been completed. In Unit-2, Civil works in regard to the erection of Scroll casing has been completed. In Unit-1, Concreting around the Knee liner upto EL 1020.50 m. has been completed. The project is scheduled for commissioning by March 2001.

III. Dhauliganga H.E. Project (280 MW): Phase-II of the Consultancy Services undertaken by M/s Electro Watt Nippon Koei, are in progress. Prequalification of contractors in regard to Main Civil works (i.e. Dam, Power House, Power Tunnel etc.), Hydro-mechanical works and Electro-mechanical works has been done. Meanwhile, the work on Diversion Tunnel has been taken up departmentally. The Project is scheduled for completion by September 2004.

IV. Koel Karo, H.E. Project (710 MW): Works of the project could not be started due to paucity of funds and local resistance. Expenditure has been accorded to the tune of Rs.20 crore, for undertaking Pre-construction activities and development of infrastructural facilities, pending investment decision.

Central Empowered Committee (CEC) recommended freezing of further expenditure on Koel Karo Project. Environmental clearance, which was accorded to this project during 1982, has recently been withdrawn by the MOE&F. The project is scheduled for completion in 7 years from the Zero date.

V. Kalpong H.E. Project (5.25 MW): Infrastructural and Pre-construction activities are in progress at this project, which has been undertaken by the Corporation as a "Deposit Work". Contract for Concrete dam, Rock Fill dam, Link channel and Saddle Dykes-I&II has been awarded. Penstock and Power House excavation works have been taken up departmentally. CAT Plan of the right fork area has been prepared and forwarded to the MOE&F for approval. The project is scheduled for completion by October 2002.

VI. Kurichu H.E. Project (45 MW): This Project is being constructed by the Corporation on a turnkey basis. Diversion Tunnel of the project has been completed and Kurichu River has been diverted in November, 1998. The work of construction of Power House was awarded to M/s Gammon India Ltd. 26,200 cum. excavation in the Power House has been achieved. In dam works out of total excavation of 359000 cum. about 97,074 cum i.e. 27%, excavation has been achieved. Design and engineering aspects, relating to the Civil and electrical works, have been progressing as per schedule. Award of contract for transmission line construction is under finalisation. The Project is scheduled for completion by September, 2001.

New schemes:

Chamera H.E. Project Stage-II (300 MW): The contract for construction of this Project on a "Turnkey Basis" is under finalisation. An expenditure sanction to the tune of Rs. 20 crore, has been accorded for undertaking pre-construction activities and development of infrastructural facilities at this Project, pending investment decision. Development of Infrastructure facilities at the Project have been started.

Teesta-V H.E. Project (510 MW): Necessary Pre-construction Investigation activities-such as drilling and drifting at the Dam and Power House sites, have been completed departmentally. TEC has been given on 23.9.1998 for a completion cost of Rs.2568.09 crore including IDC of Rs.223.40 crore. An expenditure sanction has been given to the tune of Rs.20 crore, for undertaking Pre-construction activities and development of Infrastructural facilities at this Project, pending investment decision.

Loktak Downstream H.E. Project (90 MW): The Project was Techno-economically cleared in January, 1993. Again revised TEC has been given in September, 1998 for an updated cost of Rs.557.83 cr. Including IDC of Rs.45.15 cr. at May, 1998 Price Level. An expenditure has been accorded to the tune of Rs. 13.54 crore, for undertaking pre-construction activities and development of infrastructural facilities at this project, pending investment decision.

Parbati H.E. Project Stage-II (4x200 MW), HP: The Project has earlier been accorded techno economic clearance by CEA in January, 1995 for Rs. 2151.78 crore (at June, 1994 price level) including IDC of Rs. 643.13 crore.

Investigation projects

— Dhauliganga H.E. Project (intermediate Stage) (4x50

MW), U.P.: Detailed Project Report has been submitted for issue of Techno Economic Clearance.

— Goriganga H.E. Project-(Stage IIIA & IIIB) (3 x 40 + 2x 10MW), U.P.:

— The investigation works had already been completed and the DPR submitted to Central Electricity Authority for Techno Economic Approval. However, CEA had recommended that the planning process of the project might be deferred till the Detailed Project Report of the Pancheswar Multipurpose Project is completed.

— Goriganga HE Project - (Stage IIIA & IIIB) (3x40 +2 x10 MW), U.P.: The investigation has already been completed and the Detailed Project Report has been submitted to Central Electricity Authority for Techno-Economic Clearance. UP Jal Vidyut Nigam has entrusted a small hydroelectric project of 9 MW namely Madkini HE Project, to M/s Himalaya Hydro Power Ltd. Which is a private company. This project is in conflict with these projects. As per the advice of CEA, NHPC has initiated action to resolve this issue with Jal Vidyut Nigam.

The forest proposal have not been forwarded by the State Government to MOEF. The projects are not being cleared from wildlife angle as the project area falls within the Askot Musk Deer Sanctuary. The matter has been taken up with MOEF.

Small/mini hydro electric project

The Corporation has been contemplating to undertake execution of Small/Mini Hydro Electric Projects, in order to bridge the gap between the demand and supply of electric power on one hand and to rectify the prevailing imbalance in the Hydro-Thermal mix on the other, to the best possible extent, during the 9th Five Year Plan.

Feasibility reports in respect of 4 projects located in the State of Bihar, 5 more projects located in the State of Uttar Pradesh and 3 other projects located in the State of Arunachal Pradesh, are under detailed scrutiny. Few more proposals located in the State of Tamil Nadu are also under examination.

Wind power project

After having diversified its activities, the Corporation has undertaken the execution of 25 MW. Wind Power Project in the first instance, which is located near Coimbatore (Tamil Nadu). Technical bids and price bids are under scrutiny, while "Turnkey" execution of the Project, pre-qualification bids are under evaluation.

Consultancy services

— Consultancy Services are also being renderd by the Corporation to various outside agencies:

— Tala H.E. Project Implementation Authority (Bhutan) has desired the Corporation to make Hydraulic transient Studies for Tala Project. The Scope of work and relevant inputs for undertaking the job has been finalised and work on the assignment has been started.

— NHPC is providing Design, Construction and Monitoring support services to the West Bengal Power Development Corporation Ltd. (WBPDCL) for Bakreshwar HE Project.

— Work awarded by the Border Roads Organisation to the Corporation in regard to the Concrete Lining of the Eastern Tube of the Jawahar Tunnel was successfully completed on 25.9.1998.

— The Railways have approached NHPC to provide them with Consultancy services in the detailed engineering of tunnels and cut & cover for the execution of Udhampur-Katra rail link in J&K. The final report of the investigation studies conducted by RITES have been received and based on these report the design parameters are being finalised.

Rural Electrification Corporation (REC)

Rural Electrification Corporation (REC) was set up in 1969 with the primary objective of providing financial assistance for rural electrification in the country. REC was declared a Public Financial Institution under Section 4-A of the Companies Act in 1992. In February, 1998, the Corporation was registered as a Non-Banking Financial Company under Section 45-1 A of the RBI Act, 1934. The authorised share capital of the Corporation is Rs. 800 Crore. During the year 1998-99 Government of India has contributed Rs.50 Crore towards the share capital of the Corporation increasing its paid up capital to Rs.680.60 Crore as on 30.11.1998.

Rural Electrification Programmes financed by the Corporation cover electrification of villages, including tribal villages and Dalit Bastis, energisation of pumpsets, provision of power for small, agro-based and rural industries, lighting of rural households and street lighting.

The Corporation has also been providing assistance to the State electricity boards for taking up System Improvement Projects for strengthening and improving sub-transmission and distribution system and small generation projects like wind energy and hydel projects. In addition, under Kutir Jyoti programme launched in 1988-89 by the Govt. of India, one time initial cost of internal wiring and service connection charges upto a maximum limit of Rs.1000 per connection with installation of meter or Rs.800 per connection without meter is provided to rural households below poverty line as grant through the State Govts./SEBs.

Performance highlights for 1997-98

The Corporation made the disbursement of Rs. 1093.81 Crore and made recovery of Rs.1155.57 Crore during the year 1997-98. The Corporation posted a net profit of Rs. 121 crore and paid Dividend of Rs. 10 crore for 1997-98.

Annual plan for the year 1998-99

The Annual Plan of REC for the financial year 1998-99 entails financial outlay of Rs. 1250 crore with target for electrification of 2000 villages, energisation of 2,51,000 pumpsets and release of 4.45 lakh Kutir Jyoti connections. Out of this allocation, an amount of Rs.50 crore has been earmarked for electrification of 500 tribal villages and Rs. 76 crore for electrification of Dalit Bastis.

Further, the financial allocation as above for 1998-99 also includes Rs.75 crore for funding OECF assisted projects.

Memorandum of understanding

The Corporation has signed a Memorandum of Understanding with the Ministry of Power for the current financial year 1998-99. The commitments of REG include achieving a gross margin of Rs.550 crore and realisation of Rs.900 crore of dues from the SEBs.

During 1997-98 the performance of the Corporation has been rated as "Excellent".

Issue of priority sector bonds

Govt. of India have approved raising Rs. 500 crore from the market during the fiscal year 1998-99 by way of issue of Tax-free Bonds upto Rs. 225 crore and Taxable Bonds upto Rs. 275 crore under priority sector Lending Programme. Two premier Rating Agencies viz.CRISIL and ICRA have assigned highest rating for the above issue of Bonds. The corporation has already raised Rs. 225 crores by way of Tax Free Bonds on most competitive terms.

Disbursement of loans

The Corporation disbursed a total sum of Rs.531.22 crore upto 30th November, 1998 including Kutir Jyoti Grant of Rs. 20.11 crore and energy Conservation Project Grant of Rs. 0.11 crore. The target of disbursement aggregating to Rs.1250 crore for the full year 1998-99 as provided in the Annual Plan is expected to be achieved fully

Physical progress upto 30th November, 1998

During the year 1998-99, electrification of 558 villages and energisation of 1,39,377 pumpsets have been completed upto November, 1998. A sum of Rs.20.11 crore was disbursed as Grant towards Kutir Jyoti Programme upto November, 1998. Cumulatively upto November, 1998 over 3 lakh villages have been electrified and 72 lakh pumpsets energised under REG schemes.

Rural electric cooperatives

As on 30th November, 1998, REC has sanctioned 41 RE Cooperatives in the country spread over 12 states. Of these, 33 societies are at present operative in the 6 states. Eight societies - 3 in Rajasthan and one each in Bihar, Gujarat, Orissa, Jammu and Uttar Pradesh have been liquidated over the years.

During the current financial year 1998-99 upto November, 1998, the operating societies have released a total of 11171 service connections which includes 2007 pumpsets, 360 industries and 8804 domestic/ commercial and others. The societies have also electrified 8 hamlets so far during the year 1998-99.

Cumulatively, upto the end of November, 1998, the RE Cooperatives have electrified 4171 villages, 1889 hamlets and have released 11,47,355 services, which includes 2,29,473 pumpsets, 21,909 industries and 8,95,973 domestic/commercial and other services.

During the remaining period of the current year (upto March, 99) another 4 villages and 12 hamlets are expected to be electrified and connections may be given to 3000 pumpsets, 121 industries and 12000 domestic/ commercial and other services.

OECD assistance

Under the assistance of 24.4 billion Yen (Rs.760 crore @ exchange Rate of 1 Re=3.21 Yen) sanctioned by Overseas Economic Cooperation Fund Japan (OECF) for utilisation within the extended validity period of Feb., 2002,21 system improvement Sub-project under the current batch involving an outlay of Rs. 108 crore in the States of Andhra Pradesh, Haryana, Karnataka, West Bengal are under implementation. Twelve Subprojects have been completed. Six sub-projects are scheduled for completion by March, 1999, 2 subprojects are scheduled for completion by June, 1999, and 1 sub-project is scheduled for completion by Sept., 1999.

An amount of R8.110 crore has been disbursed under OECF assistance so far (upto 9.12.98) including Rs.45 crore during the current financial year 1998-99 covering 5 states of Andhra Pradesh, Haryana, Karnataka, West Bengal & Kerala.

In addition to the current batch of sub-projects, OECF has additionally approved 20 system improvement subprojects for Rs.362 crore in the States of Andhra Pradesh, Kerala & Orissa and one small Hydro Electric Sub-project for Rs. 13 crore in Tamil Nadu. Work is in progress for the 17 sub-projects and is scheduled for completion by Dec., 2000.

To utilise the assistance in full, REC has posed 9 new sub-projects involving utilisation of Rs.254 crores in the States of Maharashtra, Karnataka and Kerala. The subprojects have been appraised by OECF Appraisal Mission.

Central Institute for Rural Electrification (CIRE)

CIRE continued to organise several All India and Regional Level Training Programmes and Workshops attracting participants from SEBs, Govt. Depts., Rural Cooperatives besides Corporation's own officers. During October, 1998, CIRE conducted a National Workshop for Chief Project Managers of different Project offices and other senior officers of REC on Review of RE Programmes.

On renewable energy systems, three programmes were conducted, one on "SPV Water Pumps" in October 1998 and two in November, 1998 on "SPV design and Engineering" and "Orientation Programme to Mahila NGOs and social Workers" on Renewable Energy Systems. Each programme was attended by more than 30 participants from different organisations. The programme for Mahila NGOs and Social Workers was conducted for the first time to give exposure on renewable energy systems and to help promote the role of women in entrepreneurship which was sponsored by IREDA.

Two technical programmes one on "Distribution Transformers for Power utilities" with 17 participants and one on "Energy Audit and Demand side management" with 8 participants were conducted during November and December, 1998 respectively. A training programme on "Application of Commercial Accounting System in SEBs" was also conducted during December, 1998. 21 participants attended the programme.

CIRE is contemplating to conduct seminars on Rural Electrification topics in the near future besides planning to conduct Energy Conservation Programmes which will be sponsored by Ministry of Power (Government of India). In addition, CIRE has scheduled six more Training Programmes upto March, 1998.

As a part of consultancy work, CIRE has submitted reports to Kerala Electricity Board on planning and formulation of district-wise integrated System Improvement Schemes for 11 districts. The institute also supplied application software.

Standardisation of equipment construction practices and research and development

The Corporation continued its drive towards standardisation of equipment material and construction practices for RE Programmes including introduction for innovative technologies with special emphasis on energy conservation. So far 308 standards comprising 74 specifications for equipment/material and 234 construction practices have been evolved and issued by the corporation.

The National level Committee constituted under the Chairmanship of CMD, REC and comprising top ranking technical experts and representatives for SEBs, Bureau of Indian Standards (BIS), Research Institutions and Transformer Manufacturers, after series of meeting and intense deliberations, finalised the report containing the Action Points/Recommendations for reducing the failure rate of the transformers and improving their performance in a time bound manner. Further follow-up action has been initiated by formulating working groups for revision of REC specifications on distribution transformers and circuit breaker on I.T. Side of distribution transformers in line.

In addition, draft specifications on Single Phase and Three Phase static Watt Hours Meters have been discussed in the meetings of the working group held in May, 1998 and August, 1998.

New thrust area— financing of small generation projects

In view of the importance of renewable energy

technologies in the context of power supply to rural areas, REC has been making efforts to promote and utilise renewable energy resources in keeping with the twin objectives of (i) electrification of villages, particularly those villages which are in interior and far-off locations and are not feasible for grid extension; and (ii) augmentation of power supply on decentralised concept. Among various renewable energy sources, location specific small hydel - wind energy cogeneration projects offer opportunities to supplement rural power whereas biomass gasifiers, mini/micro hydel projects and SPV systems can be gainfully utilised for electrification of villages based on locally available energy resources in a cost effective manner.

Rural Electrification Corporation has firmed up the procedures and guidelines for financing of small generation projects to state owned bodies, private entrepreneurs, and cooperative societies in the country. Presently small hydel and bio gas based cogeneration of power are identified as priority sector. The efforts are also under way for financing of wind energy projects by REC. A 'Business Meet' with wind energy manufacturers was held at Chennai in August, 1998 to explore possibility for financing of wind energy projects based on workable financial model. REC has also been making efforts for application of SPV technologies for the purpose of household lighting and water pumping systems.

During the year 1998-99 four small generation projects namely (i) Malankara small hydel (10.5 MW capacity), Kerala (ii) Korba Thermal tail end (1000 KW), MP (iii) Diesel generation augmentation Leh (2 MW), J&K and (iv) Diesel renovation Kargil, J&K have been sanctioned so far involving a total loan assistance of Rs.41 crore.

North Eastern Electric Power Corporation (NEEPCO)

The North Eastern Electric Power Corporation Ltd. (NEEPCO) was constituted in 1976 under the company's act 1956 with the objective of developing the large power potential of the North Eastern Region of the country through planned development of power generation projects which in turn would effectively promote the development of the North Eastern Region.

Since then NEEPCO has grown into one of the pioneer public sectors with an authorised share capital of Rs.2500.00 cr. It is a Schedule "B" organisation.

The North Eastern Region of the country is blessed with highest hydro-power potential of the country which is estimated at 48000 MW constituting about 33% of the total reserves of the country. The region has abundant natural gas reserves. There is ample scope of development in this under developed region where the main infrastructure has been identified as power.

The main objectives of the North Eastern Electric Power Corporation are to add to the power generating capacity in the North Eastern Region by installing hydro and thermal power plants to ensure optimum utilisation of commissioned generation projects, to generate adequate internal resources by ensuring justifiable return on investment and to continue sustained efforts to obtain the receivable from State Electricity Boards/ Departments; to undertake long terms feasibility studies for optimum development of Hydro Power resources of river basins in North Eastern Region.

Out of a total installed capacity of 1649 MW (Grid) in the North Eastern Region, NEEPCO is contributing 625 MW through its Kopili H.E. Projects, (250 MW) N.C. Hills, Assam, Assam gas Based Power project (291 MW), Khatalguri & Agartala Gas Turbine Power Project,

(84MW) Tripura, under O&M. During 1998-99 NEEPCO has been able to synchronise last ST Unit of 30 MW of AGBPP and last G.T. Unit of 21 MW of AGTR Inspite of having only 37.9% of the total installed capacity in the region, the Corporation has been able to meet more than 40% of the peak demand/energy needs of the region.

The Corporation achieved a capacity addition of 251 MW within the VIIIth Five Year Plan and another 173 MW in the year 1997-98, 51 MW in the year 1998-99.

In 1999-2000 a capacity addition of 50 MW has been targeted to be achieved. The corporation proposes a capacity addition of 405 MW of Ranganadi H.E. Project (on-going) and 25 MW of Doyang H.E. Project (on-going) and 25 MW of Kopili stage-II project, during remaining period of IXth Plan.

The Corporation has also taken up Tuirial H.E. Project of 60 MW in the State of Mizoram with OECF funding, which is scheduled to be completed in 2006. In addition to above assistance the Corporation is negotiating with different State Govts. of North eastern Region to take up the following projects.

— Lower Kopili H.E. Project, Assam - 150 MW

— Tuivai H.E. Project, Mizoram - 210 MW

— Kameng H.E. Project, Arunachal Pradesh-600 MW

Several other projects as mentioned below are also being proposed to be taken up during IXth Plan:

— Ranganadi H.E. Project - Stage-II, Arunachal Pradesh - 180 MW

— Kolodyne H.E. Project, Mizoram - 90 MW

— Sissiri H.E.Project, Arunachal Pradesh - 225 MW

— Tipaimukh H.E. Project, Manipur - 1500 MW

Power projects under operations & maintenance (completed)

— *Kopili H.E. Project (150 MW)-Assam:* Kopili H.E. Project (150 MW) is located in N.C. Hills district of Assam and was completed in March'98 at a cost of Rs.243.82 cr. It is a twin project consisting of two Dams two Water Conductor Systems leading from the Kopili reservoir to the Khandong Power House (2x25 MW) and from Umrong reservoir to the Kopili Power House (2x50 MW) This project started commercial generation from June/July 1988.

— *Kopili H.E. Project 1st Stage Extension (100 MW), Assam:* This is an Extension of the Kopili Project by addition of one more Penstock and extension of the existing power House Building for installation of 2x50 MW generation capacity costing Rs.134.48 crs.(including IDC). This extention will add another 502 MU of energy annually at 90% dependable year. 1st unit(called Unit-III) was synchronised on 5.3.97 and 2nd (called Unit-IV) was synchronised on 17.6.97.

— Assam Gas Based Combined Cycle Power Project (291 MW) -Assam This project is located in Dibrugarh district of Upper Assam. It was administratively approved during Nov. 1984 at a cost Rs.203.17 crs. for installing 6 Units of 33.5 MW each Gas Turbine and 3 Units of 30 MW each Steam Turbine. The project cost has been subsequently revised. The latest revised cost after completion during 1998-99 comes to Rs.1532.32 crs. Including IDC at 1998 price level.

— Agartala Gas Turbine Power Project (84 MW) Tripura This project is located in West Tripura District of Tripura. The project envisages installation 4 Gas Turbine units of 21 MW each at a cost of Rs.294.05 crs.(including IDC). The completed cost of the project has gone upto Rs.322.50 crs. as against the lates cost estimate of Rs.294.05 crs. The project is fully commissioned in June' 1998.

Power generation

During 1998-99, generation of power upto 30.11.98 was 778.32 MU against a target of 1017.00 MU by Hydro Power Stations and 569.60 MU against a target of 636.00 MU by Thermal Power Stations.

The cumulative generation since inception till Nov.'1998 in respect of Kopili H.E. Project is 8198.34 MU and 715.40 MU by Kopili H. E. Project -1 st Stage Extension, and 1994.00 MU by Kathalguri Gas Turbine Power Project and 162.50 MU by Agartala Gas Turbine Power Project.

Project wise anticipated target to be achieved during the remaining period of the year 1998-99 i.e. from Dec'98 to March'99 are given below:

— Kopili H.E. Project 134 MU

— Kopili H.E. Project-1st Stage Extension 63.50 MU

— Assam Gas Based Power Project 441 MU

— Agartala Gas Turbine Power Project 123 MU

On-going projects (generation):

— *Doyang H.E. Project (75 MW)-Nagaland:* This project is located in the Wokha district of Nagaland. The project was administratively approved in July' 1989 for installing 3 units of 25 MW. The latest cost of the project at Feb'1993 price level was Rs.384.75 cr. (including IDC) and CCEA clearance was obtained in August' 1995. The latest anticipated cost of the project of Rs.671.22 Cr. (including IDC) at June, 1998 price level has been submitted for approval.

— *Ranganadi H.E. Project (405 MW) - Arunachal Pradesh:*

The project is located in the Lower Subansiri District of Arunachal Pradesh and has a provision of installing 3 units of 135 MW each with zero date as 05/87. The cost of the project was Rs. 774.12 cr.(including IDC) at February, 1993 price level and the same has been approved in August, 1995. The project envisages to generate 1874 MU annually at rated capacity. The project is expected to be fully commissioned by 2000 to 2001.

The anticipated revised cost of the project of Rs. 1265.02 cr. (including IDC) at Sept '98 price level has been submitted for approval.

— Tuirial H.E. Project (60 MW)-Mizoram: The Tuirial H.E. Project in Mizoram is located on the border of Chachar District of Assam and Aizwal District of Mizoram and comprises construction of a 77 M high Homogenous Earth fill Dam across the Tuirial river with an installed capacity of 2x30 MW, surface power House on the left bank of the river. The completed cost of the Project at Dec'96 price level is Rs. 448.19 crs. The PIB clearance was obtained on 27.1.98 and CCEA clearance has also been accorded on 7.7.98.

— It is proposed to take up the project as a Central Sector Scheme under loan assistance of OECF, Japan with 85% of the project cost being financed under OECF loan assistance and balance 15% from Govt. of India's assistance.

— *Kopili H.E. Project-Stage-II (25 MW)-Assam:* During the construction of the 1st Stage of the Kopili H.E. Project, it was found feasible to set up a second Power House at Khandong with an installed capacity of 1x25 MW named as 2nd stage. The proposed location of the Power House is near the existing Khandong Power House. The scheme consists of a bypass tunnel of length 325 M. from Khandong, one 2.75 Media. Penstock, a surface Power House & a tail race tunnel to release the Water into Umrong Reservoir.

— The estimated cost is Rs. 98.23 cr. at 1998 price level. Preliminary construction activities on the project have been started. The project is expected to be completed during IXth Plan and is envisaged to produce additional 301 MU per year.

Power Finance Corporation (PFC)

The Power Finance Corporation Ltd. (PFC) was incorporated on 10th July, 1986 under the Companies Act, 1956. The mission of PFC is to function as the prime Development Financial Institution dedicated to the growth and overall development of the Power Sector.

The borrower-portfolio of PFC comprises the State Electricity Boards, State Generation Croporations, Municipal run power utilities besides the central and private sector power utilities.

The funds provided by the Corporation are in the nature of additionality to Plan Allocation (in respect of SEBs etc.) and based on the merits of the individual projects. As on 30th November, 1998, the Authorised Capital and the paid -up (equity) capital of the Croporation stood at Rs.2000 Crore and Rs. 1030 Crore, respectively. The Power Finance Corporation is a Schedule 'A' organisation.

Performance highlights

As on 30.11.1998, PFC sanctioned loans of the order of Rs' 2492 crore (during 1998-99) for power projects in various parts of the country and disbursements are made to the tune of Rs.1372 Crore. The PFC was placed in the highest category of 'Excellent' for the fifth time in succession on the basis of its all-round performance during the year.

Resource mobilisation (international)

In order to meet its increasing fund requirements, PFC stepped-up its efforts to tap External Commercial Borrowing (ECB) market.

Syndicated loan of US$ 100 million: In the financial year 1998-99 PFC has raised a syndicated loan of US$ 100 million at a very competitive price of 115 bppa over US$ 6 months LIBOR having a maturity period of 7 years with a put option at the end of 5 years.

Resource mobilisation- (Domestic)

During the year (upto 30,11,1998). the Corporation has raised Rs. 560.50 Crore out of which Rs.300.50 Crore by way of unsecured bonds and Rs. 250.00 Crore by way of term loan from banks. The Corporation obtained from Reserve Bank of India specific exemption in respect of the applicability of the provisions (of NBFC directions 1998). The Corporation can now raise the money by issue of unsecured bonds for a period more than 5 years w.e.f. 14th July, 1998.

Bonds: Out of the funds raised by way of unsecured bonds of Rs.300.50 Crore, Rs. 150.50 Crore has been raised by issue of Tax Free Bonds at the rate of 10.4% p.a. payable half yearly for a tenure of 10 years, Rs. 50 Crore has been raised by issue of Taxable Bonds at the rate of 13.25% p.a. payable half yearly for a tenure of 7 years.

The Corporation has also received funds of Rs. 100 Crore out of the proceeds from Resurgent India Bonds from SBI and issued Unsecured, Taxable Bonds in the nature of debentures at the rate of 12.75% p.a. payable half yearly for a tenure of 5 years. The Corporation is also planning to launch a Rs. 400 Crore taxable bonds issue on private placement basis shortly.

The Croporation has raised Rs.260 Crore i.e. Rs. 110 from SBI and Rs.150 Crore from PNB at the bank's PLR rate.

External credit utilisation

The Loan of US$ 265 million (Revised to US$ 215 Million) from World Bank for Power Utilities Efficiency Improvement Project became effective from 18.3.1997. The Corporation has sanctioned US$ 258.21 million against US$ 220 million and for Pre-investment Fund the Corporation has sanctioned US$ 36.98 million against US$ 20 million. Upto 30.11.1998 the Corporation has sent claims to Government of India equivalent to Rs. 749.03 Crore. PFC is exploring the possibility of tying up a fresh line of Credit of US$ 500 million with the World Bank.

Asian Development Bank (ADB)

The loan of US$ 250 million (revised to US$ 210 million) from ADB under Power Efficiency (Sector) Project became effective from 22,7.1997. The loan is to finance sub-projects of selected SEBs. The Corporation has sanctioned US$ 260 million against US$ 250 million and upto 30.11.1998 claims equivalent to Rs. 716.91 Crore have been submitted . PFC is currently negotiating with the ADB for a US$ 250 million loan with a T.A. component of US$ 1 million.

Overseas Development Agency (Now DFID)

The ODA of UK signed an agreement with Government of India on 17.9.1993 under Energy Efficiency Programme, under which a project of renovation and uprating of Hirakud hydro power station of Stage I Unit I and II has been approved. The funds are to be canalised through PFC. The PFC has sanctioned a sum of US$ 23.52 million and claim submitted equivalent to Rs.64.73 Crore on 30.11.1998.

Kreditanstalt Fur Wiederaufbau (KFW)

PFC signed loan agreement with KFW of Germany in June, 1995 for a mixed credit of DM 46.5 million under Energy Investment Programme, for being utilised for financing rehabilitation of existing Power Plants and distribution systems. Rehabilitation of Koyna HEP Stage I & II in Maharashtra and Hirakud HEP Stage I Unit 3 & 4 are to be covered from the loan. PFC has disbursed Rs.45.43 crore as on 30.11.1998 for Koyna HEP of MSEB.

PFC had provided Payment Guarantee to KfW on behalf of Haryana State Electricity Board (HSEB) for a loan amount of DM 138 million taken to finance imports for renovation and modernisation of Panipat TPS.

Credit rating

Subsequent to the revision of the credit rating of India, Moody's and S&P have also revised the credit rating of PFC. The Moody's rating for long-term foreign currency bonds lowered to'Ba2' (Sovereign) 'Baa3'on 6th June, 1998. The S&P downgraded the rating to BB/ stable (soveriegn) from BB+/negative on 23rd October, 1998.

Credit Rating & Information services of India (CRISIL) -has assigned the highest rating of 'FAAN for PFC's Fixed Deposit Programme. Investment Information and Credit Rating Agency (ICRA) has reaffirmed 'MAAN for PFC's Fixed Deposit Programme on 3.11.1998.

Institutional development

Operational and financial action plan

PFC has been endeavouring to improve the operational and financial health of the state power utilities through formulation and implementation of Operational and Financial Action Plan (OFAP). During 1998-99, OFAPs of Department of Power in J&K and Goa have been put in place. OFAP of HPSEB has also been revised during the year. As of now, 30 OFAPs are in place for 14 SEBs and SGCs, 1 Municipality-run utility, 5 State Electricity Departments and 1 Joint Sector Power Utility and 1 transmission utility incorporated under the Companies Act.

Some major achievements of this mechanism are:

— SEBs have started booking subsidy to achieve 3% ROR.

— Number of SEBs achieving 3% ROR has increased.

— State Governments have started releasing subsidy.

— Tariff, revisions have been frequent and of larger magnitude.

— Capital restructuring has been undertaken in most of the SEBs.

— Improvement in liquidity has been brought about through control over receivables.

— Steps have been taken for computerisation of the operations of the SEBs and to establish dedicated communication system. Also computerisation in billing has been undertaken in most of the SEBs.

— Fuel Cost Adjustment (full) has been permitted in five states and partially in some other States. Finalisation of pending accounts within the set time frame has started.

Reforms and restructing

PFC has decided to support and pursue the State Governments to restructure their power sector to: achieve commercial/operational/efficiency; improve viability/ delivery of services; achieve cost effectiveness through technical/ managerial/administrative restructuring; in crease operational efficiency through greater competition managerial autonomy and higher responsibility.

PFC has formulated a policy of providing a financial package by relaxing exposure norms for reforming states. The various State Governments have expressed their willingness and financial assistance of PFC.

Support for consultancy services

PFC provides concessional financing to the SEBs/SGCs for engaging the services of consultants to help them undertake the preparation of Pre-Feasibility Reports, detailed Feasibility Reports and Detailed Engineering for power schemes and also in the preparation, solicitation and evaluation of proposals and negotiation of Power Purchase Agreement with the Independent Power Producers. PFC is also maintaining a Data Bank of consultants to help the SEB's in hiring their services.

Tariff and project cost related studies

Under USAID sponsored EMCAT project, PFC had conducted studies regarding formulation of tariffs/ incremental tariffs for different supply and consumer segments; and study of past trend in cost to evolve a system of cost estimation of Power projects.

Accelerated Generation and Supply Programme (AG&SP)

Accelerated Generation and Supply Programme was launched by PFC with the approval of the Cabinet in September, 1997. The target of PFC disbursements under the programme during the financial year 199798 was Rs. 1050 Crores against which actual achievement of Rs. 1270 Crores was 20% higher.

The interest subsidy on this disbursement is Rs.240 Crores (against Rs.200 Crores provided for in the budget). The financial assistance from PFC has helped in addition of 676 MW during the financial year 1997-98. Government has approved, in July, 1998, the proposal for continuation of the Accelerated Generation and Supply

Programme (AG&SP) during the remaining period of the Ninth Plan through the Power Finance Corporation (PFC) to State Electricity Boards/State Generation Corporations/State Power Departments and Central Utilities.

Streamlining activities pertaining to R&M and life extension studies and works

To accelerate the R&M the Life Extension Works of old thermal power stations in India, initiatives have also been taken by PFC in close consultation with SEBs/ States and CEA. Normal eligibility conditions and exposure limits to finance R&M schemes of even SEBs ineligible to avail PFC loans with appropriate loan conditions. Task Force was set up in July, 1997 with members from CEA, BHEL, Planning Commission and PFC to accelerate R&M projects implementation. CEA and BHEL Roving Teams have visited the SEBs and reviewed the R&M activities required on various TPS included in R&M Phase 11 (8th Plan). PFC in association with SEBs has initiated the action for short-listing and registration of vendors for undertaking R&M and LE studies/works on aged/ageing coal based thermal power stations in India.

Design and setting up of model distribution management system

The commercial losses of electricity which is identified as main cause of losses of SEBs can be controlled through improved distribution management and accountability. PFC has identified design and setting up of nodal Distribution Management System (DMS) in each SEB as a very high priority. PFC is working to provide interest free loan or grant for study and analysis in one selected distribution area typical for the State (Phase 1) and also to provide soft loan for implementation of the recommendation of Phase I study to set up DMS to achieve economical investment to enhance revenue stream.

Contribution to physical achievement through PFC financing

PFC's financial assistance have cumulatively helped in installation of 8102 MVAR Shunt Capacitors; additional generation of 4240 million units per annum through Renovation and Modernisation of Thermal Power Plants; addition of 402 MW by way of restoration of capacity and additional generation of 364 million units per annum through Renovation and Uprating of Hydro Power Plants; addition of 10125 MW of Thermal Generation and 961 MW of Hydel Generation capacity by way of completion of on going generation projects; addition of 18507 Ckt.Kms. of transmission lines and 25215 MVA transformation capacity through Transmission schemes; 4458 Ckt.Kms. of transmission lines, 4671 MVA transformation capacity and 938 MVAR capacitors through Urban Distribution schemes, till March, 1998.

Participation in private projects

PFC decided to expand its borrowers portfolio to include private sector borrowers. PFC has so far sanctioned 8 loans worth about Rs.941 Crore including Rs. 47.50 Crore sanctioned to BSES for improvement of T&D system in Maharashtra, Rs. 212 crore for Maheshwar HEP in Madhya Pradesh, Rs. 150 Crore for Mangrol TPS of M/s GIPCL in Gujarat, Rs.170 Crore for Kondapalli Power Corporation Limited in Andhra Pradesh and Rs. 210 Crore for Jaiprakash Hydro Power Ltd. Mostly, PFC works in consortium with other FIs like IDBI, ICICI, IFCI for financing private power projects.

Financing working capital requirements

PFC has decided to provide finance against Working Capital requirements of state utilities. The scheme covers all existing borrowers in the State Sector who are not declared as defaulters by PFC at any point of time in the 12 months preceding the month in which the application for Working Capital Loan is received by PFC. The

Corporation has so far sanctioned an amount of Rs. 180 Crore and disbursed the same.

Leasing scheme for power equipment

PFC had recently introduced financial leasing of power equipment such as generators, turbines, transformers, capacitors and any defined portion of a power projects to the entities in power sector. All entities in state sector, municipalbodies, private sector, joint sector engaged in power generation, transmission and distribution, energy conservation, R&M etc. and associated sectors are eligible for funds under this scheme. PFC has sanctioned an amount of Rs. 285 Crore under this scheme and disbursed an amount of Rs. 280 Crore.

Direct discounting of bills scheme

The credit under this scheme is available to all equipment manufacturers to enable them to sell their equipment on deferred payment terms to the purchasers in power sector. The scheme covers sale of machinery, capital goods and turnkey projects. Extent of assistance under this scheme is available upto 100% of the invoice value including insurance, freight and taxes. The Corporation has so far sanctioned an amount of Rs. 50 Crore under this scheme.

Customer orientation

PFC has been, from time to time, organising meetings with the Chairman of state power utilities, Energy Secretaries and other senior officials from State Governments to evolve a common strategy to reorient the operations of PFC vis-a-vis state utilities for a mutually beneficial relationship and faster growth.

High level advisory committees on power and financial operations

A high level advisory committee of professionals and

experts was set up by PFC in November, 1995 under the Chairmanship of Shri V.G.Rajadhyaksha, with a view to shape up the future policies and strategies of PFC so as to improve its operations in power sector. The first report of the Committee has been submitted to PFC during January, 97 covering the following four major areas of power sector operations:

— The role of PFC in power sector operations in the emerging scenario;

— On-going generation projects;

— R&M of Thermal and Hydro power stations; and

— System Improvement in Transmission and Distribution areas;

PFC has already started implementation of these recommendations.

Another high level committee on financial operations under the Chairmanship of Shri M. Narasimhan, former Governor of Reserve Bank of India, had been set up in 1995 for fund mobilisation and deployment, financial services and instruments and possible areas for diversification. The Committee submitted their report. The majority of recommendations have been accepted for implementation and certain issues like conversion of PFC into an Financial Institution, introduction of new business activities such as credit rating, Business with other countries, etc. referred for guidance. PFC has been advised to initiate further action.

Future perspective

PFC is striving to emerge as the nodal agency through which all credits to Power Sector from bilateral/ multilateral sources, would be channelled. PFC would also endeavour to facilitate structural reforms in the State Power Sector to make it commercially viable and efficient. The PFC is in the process of finalising its Corporate Plan covering the 9th Plan period. As against a disbursement of Rs.2026 Crore during 1997-98, PFC envisages to reach annual disbursement level of about Rs.5,000 Crore by the end of 9th Plan.

Besides providing term finance to its borrowers, PFC had recently added lease finance, bill discounting; bill rediscounting, guarantee services, and consortium/ syndicate financing to its portfolio. The range of financial services may be progressively broadened in future to include fund based services such as supplier's credit, bridge finance etc. and non-fund based services such as project consultancy, financial advisory services, loan syndication and consortium financing.

Power grid corporation of India (Powergrid)

Powergrid was established in October 23,1989 with the mandate to "Establish and operate Regional and National Power Grids to facilitate transfer of power within and across the Regions with reliability, security and economy on sound commercial principles" as its mission. Powergrid's persistent efforts to accord the deserved priority to the transmission sector, which has so far eluded this vital sector of India has been recognised and powergrid has been statutorily acknowledged as Central National Transmission Utility of the country.

Powergrid's achievements

During the last 7 years, the company h as added around 13,000 ckt kms EHV transmission lines to the national network. Asset base of the company grew from Rs. 3,521 crore in 1992-93 to Rs. 8,096 crore in 1997-98, and turnover from a modest Rs.634 crore in 1992-93 to Rs.1,434.68 crore in 1997-98, registering an average annual growth rate of 21 %.

Powergrid operates over 31,000 ckt kms of

transmission lines comprising 400 KV, 220 KV, 132 KV AC transmission lines and HVDC transmission system, crisscrossing the entire length and breadth of the country with a total installed transformation capacity of around 28,000 MVA distributed over 55 sub-stations and maintained at a persistent level of over 98% of line availability, which is comparable with the best of internation standards.

Presently, Powergrid has been managing to transfer the power on an average of about 1,000 MW (maximum upto 1,880 MW), amounting to over 22 million units per day.

Business development

Based upon the in-house expertise developed in the area of engineering, contracting, project management, financial & personnel management in the transmission sector, Powergrid has bagged various vital assignments amounting to Rs.35 crore out of which Rs.13.86 crore have been realised in 1997-98. This includes Rs. 1.6 crore in Foreign exchange.

Powergrid in association with EPDCI, Japan & TEPSCO, Japan has secured an OECF funded assignment from WBSEB for Review Engineering Consultancy Services for Strengthening of Transmission System of West Bengal against stiff international competition.

Powergrid and Lahmeyer International, Germany, has jointly submitted the bids to GRIDCO, Orissa for a consultancy assignment of upgradation and reconductoring of the existing transmission lines for higher capacity of power flows.

Powergrid has been awarded the work of exclusive O&M of 400 KV, 660 cKMs of transmission lines by Karnataka Electricity Board. Powergrid has also been entrusted with the consultancy service for execution of transmission lines and substations by Pondicherry Electricity Department. Powergrid is also providing consultancy services to Energy Management Centre for Narmada Control Authority and Load Despatch and SCADA System to Bombay Suburban Electricity Supply Ltd. Powergrid has also taken various types of consultancy assignments for HPSEB, DVB and KEB.

Business opportunities are also being explored in neighbouring countries such as Nepal, Bangladesh and other Middle-east countries.

Development of national grid

Powergrid has initiated an action plan, in phased manner, to establish inter-regional links connecting all the five regions to establish a strong National Grid and integrated operation of Indian power system, as a whole.

In Phase-II, all regional grids are planned to be interconnected asynchronously (through HVDC Back to Back links), which are comparatively robust and through which controlled exchange of power is feasible even under varied system operating conditions of the connecting regions. National grid would be further strengthened in Phase-II and Phase-III with large inter-regional links planned with mega size multistate projects.

At present, powergrid has inter-connected Northern and Western Regions through a HVDC B/B link of 500 MW at Vindhyachal and inter-connected Western and Southern Regions through HVDC B/B link of 1,000 MW at Chandrapur. While the former has been generally used to exchange power to the extent of 400-500 MW in off peak hours, the later has enabled transfer of about 600-700 MW to Southern region from Western, Eastern and Northern Region.

Further, during Phase-I, Powergrid intends to connect all the Regional grids with HVDC back-to-back links that would constitute the basic structure of National Powergrid. Powergrid is implementing two HVDC B/B link (500 MW), inter-regional links in next few years. These include Gazuwaka HVDC B/B link (500 MW), inter-connecting Eastern and Southern Regions (through Jeypore-Gazuwaka 400 kV D/c line) and Sasaram HVDC B/B link (500 MW), inter-connecting Eastern and Northern Region (through Sasaram-Biharshariff 400 kV D/c line).

Under Phase-II, Powergrid proposes to further strengthen HVDC links with AC inter-regional links and creating transmission highways through mega size multistate projects (HVDC links) in next 5 to 7 years time.

Under Phase-III, the huge hydro potential in North-Eastern Region and concentration of coal reserves in states of Orissa, Bihar and Madhya Pradesh would be optimally utilised. Powergrid proposes to create very strong AC 800 kV trunk network. The systems envisaged during this phase are likely to be implemented during next ten years time.

The above plans would synchronize operation of Northern Region, North Eastern Region, Eastern Region and Western Region while Southern Region is preferred to be operated in a synchronous mode to avoid very large synchronous grid.

The exchange capacity amongst the regions will be enhanced to 4,000 MW next year. This exchange capacity will get augmented to 13,000 MW in next 5 years and will be further elevated to 30,000 MW.

Unified load despatch & communication facilities

Powergrid has undertaken implementation of state-of-the-art Unified Load Despatch and Communication facilities throughout the country. Powergrid will be investing around Rs.2,000 crores for augmentation of LD&C facilities in all the five power regions. This will facilitate consistency in design, implementation, maintenance, compatible equipment & systems and fully dedicated integrated communication network throughout the nation.

At present the implementation of LD&C facilities is in progress in Southern & Northern Regions. Powergrid is seeking the services of pioneer international consultants to help in timely execution of such projects. Contracts for all the EMS/SCADA and Communication packages under Northern & Southern Region Load Despatch & communication projects have been awarded and the projects are expected to be completed by turn of the century. Other such projects for the North-Eastern, Eastern and Western regions, are to be commissioned progressively.

Technology

Powergrid is constantly striving to improve its technology and technological know-how. Powergrid has also established a chair at IIT Delhi for Powergrid system study and thus has endeavoured to link industry and academics.

Powergrid has designed transmission towers for different wind/ice conditions, marshy/water logged and mid-steam locations besides special towers for river and power line crossings. Engineering expertise includes implementation of 400 KV AC transmission system and highly specialised areas of 300 KV AC systems, 500 KV HVDC bipole and Back-to-Back systems.

Powergrid employs state-of-the-art techniques like Hotline maintenance, Condition monitoring EHV equipments, Thermovision scanning to ensure maximum line availability without interruptions which reflects excellence in operational and maintenance expertise of the organisation, as transmission system availability is over 98% comparable to international standards.

Transmission systems are vulnerable to natural calamities like storm, tornado, land-slide, flashflood, etc. Recent devastation caused by cyclone in Gujarat in June, 1998 which disrupted the power supply network across the State was attended by Powergrid on war footing. Power supply was restored to major cities including supply of power to Kandla Port, GAIL, IOL etc. This demonstrated Powergrid's capabilities in disaster management using Emergency Restoration System.

Research and development

Detailed simulator studies were conducted at GEC, Alsthom, U.K. to verify that there is no adverse interaction between the Chandrapur HVDC Back-to-Back project of Powergrid and Chandrapur-Padghe HVDC bipolar project of MSEB. These studies were carried out using the Real Time Digital simulator (RTDS), the latest tool which was used to perform large scale simulation of Electrical Power Systems of Western and Southern Region and implemented actual control hardware of Chandrapur Back-to-Back and Chandrapur-Padghe HVDC bipole. This was the first time in the world, that such extensive studies involving two HVDC projects nearby were conducted using RTDS. M/s GEC Alsthom, ABB, HOI, BHEL, MSEB and Powergrid were involved in these studies.

Powergrid has taken up study of measurement of AC/DC fields under UHV transmission lines and in the sub-stations in association with CPRI. Also a study on possible biological effects of electric field has been taken up. The resulting data has confirmed the suitability of various design parameters in use in Powergrid. Further, means of reduction of the electric and magnetic fields have been suggested as a fall out from the studies conducted.

For the first time in India, Flexible AC Transmission System (FACTS) is proposed to be applied on 400 KV system. Towards this, Kanpur-Ballabhgarh corridor in Northern region has been identified and the project is being taken up as an R&D project in association with CPRI, BHEL and CEA.

Real Time Digital Simulator (RTDS) is being developed indigenously in association with IIT, Kharagpur which will be capable of simulating the behaviour of power system under normal and contingency conditions in real time for smooth, efficient and reliable operation as well as to train the system dispatcher/operation and other personnel.

Assisting the SEBs

Powergrid has endeavoured to extend its expertise and assistance to ameliorate transmission and distribution networks of state electricity boards which on account of financial constraints have not been able to invest in improving their system due to inadequate shunt compensation,

Powergrid has tied up financial assistance for procurement and erection of Shunt Capacitors in the state networks so as to help them in overcoming the existing deficiencies. This offer has been extended to all the SEBs in the country and procurement actions have been initiated for implementation of such schemes in different states in a phased manner.

Powergrid has undertaken maintenance of Delhi Vidyut Board Sub-stations on Management basis from May, 1998. The substations include Okhla 220 KV, Mehrauli 220 KV and Masjid Moth 33 KV. Further, Capacitors to the tune of 150 MVA been installed in 11 substations which will substantially improve the voltage and regular supply of power being fed by these substations.

Action is being initiated to meet the capacitor requirement of Punjab, Haryana and Rajasthan State Electricity Boards by way of procuring around 1,000 MVAR capacity on their behalf. While Shunt Capacitors shall continue to be under the domain of SEBs, powergrid's endeavour is to overcome the prevailing backlog on no-profit-no loss basis.

Towards green environ

Powergrid is sensitive to environmental issues and social concerns. It has evolved Environmental and Social Policy and Procedures (ESPP) within broad framework of laws, policies, constitutional commitments and responsibilities.

Powergrid is the only organisation in the power sector which has finalised its ESPP policy in consultation with public. Powergrid, inter-alia, carries out social and environmental assessment of its projects to evolve an appropriate project-specific Environmental and social Management Plan and make it an integral part of the project execution process. The three key principles of Powergrid's ESPP are Avoidance, Minimisation and Mitigation.

Sharing expertise for national benefit

Powergrid is consciously working on disseminating its experience and expertise in various facets of transmission system management to various SEBs and Electricity Departments including other Bodies in power sector through regular conferences, seminars and tailormade training programmes/workshops directed towards addressing specific technological and O&M areas. Some of the recent programmes arranged at Ballabhgarh, Delhi and Hyderabad were attended by various SEBs including representatives from Malaysia, Nepal, Bhutan, Mauritius etc. Specialised testing facilities available at Powergrid's Central Oil Testing Laboratory at Hyderabad and developmental activities carried out have resulted some of neighbouring countries like Mauritius to seek co-operation/support from powergrid. Moreover, the testing facilities are being regularly utilised by various SEBs, Generating Companies and even railways.

Powergrid's long term perspective

The long term perspective of Powergrid entails that it will be acting as a "Facilitator-cum-Change Agent" in growth and ongoing restructuring of the Indian Power Sector. An ambitious investment plan of Rs. 13,000 crore has been chalked out for the identified projects during the IXth Plan. Additional provision of Rs.5,000 crore has been earmarked for transmission lines associated with Mega IPPs. Powergrid has already planned to fund this massive investment through domestic and international borrowings as well as its internal resources.

Powergrid has been assigned the role of playing a facilitator role in establishing the mechanism for power trading through institutionalising Power Trading Corporation. This will lead the way for providing the much needed confidence to investors in the power sector on a single window basis.

Powergrid also plans to extend the power grid to the SAARC region. In a recent meeting of the SAARC countries in Dhaka, this view was re-endorsed. In this endeavour, Powergrid has acted as a catalyst to mobilise popular consent. Countries like Nepal & Bhutan are already been assisted by India for the past many years. Constant interactions are also taking place between India and Bangladesh to interconnect the countries for mutual benefit by economic exchange of power.

Powergrid will not be limiting its role to that of being only a bulk power mover but will embark into synergic areas for diversification to sustain its growth. It commits itself for playing a pivotal role in economic growth of the country by continuing to act as a dominant force in change management and as a facilitator to motivate and catalyse development in all facets of power sector.

Tehri Hydro Development Corporation (THDC)

Tehri Hydro Complex comprises the 1000 MW Tehri Dam & HPT (Stage-I), the 1000 MW pump storage plant, and the 400 MWKotesnwar Dam & HPP. Tehri Hydro Development Corporation (THDC) was incorporated on July 12th, 1988 to plan, promote, organise, execute, operate and maintain Hydro Power Projects in Bhagirathi-Bhilangna Valley in U.P. as a Joint Venture of Govt. of India and Govt. of U.P. both sharing the cost of power component (20% of Stage-1 cost) of the project in the ratio of 75: 25 respectively. The irrigation component is to be funded entirely by the Govt. of U.P.

Tehri Hydro Complex (2400 MW) was transferred to THDC by Govt. of U.P. in June 1989. Government of India on 15.3.1994 accorded approval for execution of Tehri Dam & HPP (Stage-1) alongwith the essential and committed works of Tehri Pump Storge Plant & Koteshwar Dam Project at a cost of Rs.2963.66 crs. (at March'93 price level). The revised cost estimate amounting to Rs.4982.00 crs. at Dec.'97 price level has been prepared for Tehri Stage-including committed& essential works of Koteshwar Dam and PSP and has been submitted to CEA.

Tehri Power Complex comprises of four components viz.,(1) the 260.5 M. high rock fill Tehri Dam and 1000 MW Hydro Power Plant (HPP) (Stage-I of the complex); (ii) 103.5 M. high concrete Dam with 400 MW Hydro

Power Plant at Koteshwar 22 KM downstream of Tehri; and (iii) 1000 MW Pump Storage Plant (PSP) situated just downstream of the confluence of Bhagirathi and Bhilangana river at Tehri, alongwith 800 KV Associated Transmission System for evacuation of power from the Tehri Hydro Power Complex to be executed by Power Grid Corporation of India.

It is now proposed to take up execution of the 400 MW Koteshwar Dam & HPP. Proposal for investment sanction for Koteshwar Project is presently under consideration of the Govt. Power Finance Corporation has conveyed its in-principle approval to consider term loan of Rs.560.00 crs. and other Banks have also indicated their willingness to provide loans for the project.

Project clearance

Environment Clearance was accorded to the entire Tehri Hydro Power Complex during July'90. Forest clearance was accorded to Tehri Dam & HPP during June'87. Tehri PSP does not involve any forest land. The Public Investment Board (PIB) accorded clearance to the Tehri Hydro Power Complex (2400 MW) during January'92. Clearance for the execution of Tehri Dam and HPP Staged (4x250 MW) was accorded in March'94 for the various components at an estimated cost of Rs. 3334.66 cr.(excluding IDC of Rs. 427.74 cr.) at March'93 price level. Koteshwar Dam and HPP and the Pump Storage Plant were to be taken up after funding for the same was tied up.

Benefits

Tehri Dam & HPP Staged is a Multipupose project catering to the needs of Power Generation, Irrigation and Drinking water. The main benefits from the Stage-I when completed would be:

— Addition to the installed capacity in Northern

Region:. 2400 MW (1000 MW on completion of Stage-I).

— Annual energy availability (peaking): 6500 Million Units (3568 MU on completion of Staged).

— Additional irrigation in 2.7 lacs ha. area besides stabilisation in existing 6.04 lacs Ha. area.

— 162 Million Gallons of water per day for drinking water supply to Delhi to cater to a population of 40 lacs.

— 108 Million gallons of water per day (200 cusecs) for drinking water supply to the towns and villages of Uttar Pradesh.

— Integrated development of Garhwal Region, including construction of a new hill station viz. New Tehri Town (NTT) with provision for all possible facilities, improved communication, education, health, tourist traffic, setting-up of non-polluting industries, development of horticulture, fisheries, afforestation of the region etc. much to the advantage of the people of that region.

Status of the project works (Tehari State -I)

The present status of the projects is:

— Various infrastuctural works have been completed at the project site.

— All the four diversion tunnels have been completed and the river diverted through the two right bank tunnels. Left Bank Tunnels have also been made operational.

— Excavation of four numbers head race tunnels (two each for Tehri HPP Stage -I & Tehri PSP) of 8.5 M diameter each with a total length of 5190 M. have been completed and lining work is complete in

Staged tunnels while it is partly done in tunnels for PSP. The balance works are in progress.

— The foundation of the Main Dam over the entire length of 1.1 Km. has been laid and the Main Dam raised upto 15 M above the river bed level.

— The Coffer Dam, which would from part of the Main Dam, has been raised up EL 661 M.

— The major Civil Works of Power House Complex, Main Dam and Spillways are presently under execution, and the status is as under:

Power house civil works

The work on the three packages of Power House Complex is in progress. Excavation of Machine Hall is presently under progress. Excavation of Transformer Hall has been completed. Work on Tail Race Tunnels, Drainage galleries & other faces under different packages of Power House Complex are also progressing.

DAM

Work on the 260.0 M. dam, which would be the highest rockfill dam in the Asian Region, has been taken up after it was awarded in January'97. After completion of core stripping works, raising of Main Dam is in full swing.

Spillways

Contract for major package for spillways have been awarded, and work on various fronts has started.

E & M equipment

Contracts for Turbine, Generator, Valves and Control Systems with financing have been awarded to the consortium of manufacturers from Russia/Ukraine, and ABB-Germany. The contract for EME have come into force w.e.f. 20.11.97 for HPI, Moscow, and for EME Russia on 21.1.98. The contract for ABB-Germany has come into effect on 19.3.98. Work under the contracts is; under progress. Model test on turbine has since been conducted in Dec.'98 at Kharkov plant, Ukraine.

Tenders under ICB with compulsory minimum 85% financing for other Power House equipment, viz. Transformers, Busducts, Switchgear have been invited. Techno-Commercial Bids were opened in Nov.'98 and evaluation of the bids is under progress.

Contract for various other packages viz. EOT Cranes, Penstock fabrication, Dam Instrumentation, balance Electro mechanical equipment and hydro, mechnical equipment etc. are under various stages of processing.

Rehabilitation

Rehabilitation is being implemented in two phases. Phase-I covers those families which are affected by construction of Coffer Dam including the Old Tehri Town. In Phase-II, all remaining families affected by construction of Main Dam would be rehabilitated.

The phase-I Rural Rehabilitation is nearly completed, with 98.5% of the families having been paid compensation and rehabilitated. In Phase-II, 435 out of 2845 rural families have been rehabilitated and land for the balance families in Hardwar/Dehradun areas is being acquired. The entire Phase-II affected population would be rehabilitated well before the impoundment of the reservoir.

The Urban affected population are being rehabilitated in New Tehri Town at Rishikesh/Dehradun at their option. The NTT has been developed at a height of 1350-1850 M., and has all modern facilities including a University Campus, Hospital, Institutions, Markets, Places of worship and public utility buildings.

Environment

Ministry of Environment and Forests laid down certain conditions as per studies which were to be carried out and based on their findings, action plans had to be drawn up for execution pari-passu with construction of the project. All the required studies have been completed and reports submitted to the MOEF. It has been established that there would be no adverse effect on the environment and bio-diversity of the area due to Tehri Project. THDC is carrying out Catchment Area Treatment in the high and very high erodibility classification. Around 31,000 Ha. Area has been treated so far. MOEF granted forest clearance in June, 1997 with the stipulation that the project authorities will carry out compensatory afforestation in an area of 3815 Ha. of non forest land. An area of 4516 Ha. has already been planted in the districts of Jhansi and Lalitpur in U.P. The plantation done on non-forest land is now being converted into reserve forest.

Koteshwar project

Koteshwar Project consists of a 97.5 M. high concrete dam with a surface power house at the toe of the dam, housing four units of 100 MW each with Francis type turbines. Necessary access and major infrastructure required to start the Koteshwar project is already established. Before construction of the dam, a diversion tunnel of 8M.Diameter and of 582.0 M length would be constructed to divert the flow of river. Work on this diversion tunnel has been taken up. The construction period of the project is 5 years.

Pumb Storage Plant (PSP)

Tehri PSP has been envisaged to generate 1000 MW of peaking power for enhancing system reliability and also to provide balancing load to the thermal base generation during off peak hours. Reservoir created by the Tehri

Dam would function as the upstream reservoir for this project. Koteshwar Dam will create a balancing reservoir to regulate the releases from Tehri Reservoir. Koteshwar Dam will also serve as the downstream reservoir for the PSP.

Certain essential works of PSP were taken up alongwith the execution of Stage-I works. Excavation of HFIT for both Stage-I and PSP has been completed. While lining work is completed in Staged tunnels, and partly done in PSP tunnels.

The intakes for HRT for PSP are being constructed alongwith Stage-I works. The PSP envisages 4 reversible units of 250 MW each. The main feature of the project is the variation of about 90 M. between the maximum and minim m head, under which the reversible units shall operate. This would require specialised studies to firm up the design and specfication of the pump turbine units.

Further, studies would be required for optimising the integrated operation of the three stages of the complex, viz. Tehri Staged, PSP and Koteshwar. Action is being taken to get the necessary studies conducted and firming up the design and parameters.

Nathpa Jhakri Power Corporation (NJPC)

The Nathpa Jhakri Power Corporation Limited (NJPC) was incorporated in May 24, 1988 as a joint venture of the Government of India and the Government of Himachal Pradesh with the objective to plan, promote, organise and execute Hydro-electric Power Projects in the Satluj river basin in the Himachal Pradesh. The authorised share capital of NJPC is Rs. 2200 crore.

The World Bank has sanctioned a loan of US $ 437 million for part financing of the project. The project is to be financed in 1:1 debt equity ratio. The equity portion is to be shared between Govt. of India (GOI) and Govt. of

Himachal Pradesh (GOHP) in the ratio of 3:1 respectively. In the implementation of its first project, NJPC is supported by CWC and CEA as the Principal Consultants, along with the consortium of Nippon Koei, Japan; Electrowatt, Switzerland; and WAPCOS, India, as the retainer Consultants. Besides these, NJPC is also backed by the services of a Panel of Experts, comprising both nationally/internationally renowned professionals and an Advisor (Environment/Resettlement & Rehabilitation).

Nathpa Jhakri Hydroelectric Power Project (6 x 250 MW)

The Nathpa Jhakri Hydroelectric Power Project envisages the construction of:

— A 60.50 m. high concrete Dam on Satluj river at Nathpa to divert 405 cusecs of water through four Intakes.

— An underground Desilting Complex, comprising four chambers, each 525 m. long, 16.31 m. wide and 27.5 m. deep, is one of the largest underground complex in the World.

— A 10.15 m. dia. and 27.3 km. long Head Race Tunnel (one of the longest hydro power tunnel in the world), terminating in a 21 m. dia and 301 m. deep Surge Shaft.

— Three circular steel-lined Pressure Shafts, each of 4.9 m. dia. and 633 m. long bifurcating near the Power House to feed six generating units.

— An underground Power House with a cavern size of 222 m. x 20 m. x 49 m. having six Francis Units of 250 MW each to utilise a design discharge of 405 cusecs; and design head of 425 m.

— A 10. 15 m. dia. and 982 m long Tail Race Tunnel to discharge the water back into the river satluj.

Project cost

The approved cost of the NJHPP was Rs. 4337.95 crores at March, 1993 price level. The Project is now estimated to cost Rs. 7666.31 crore at June, 1998 price level,

Project commission schedule

All the six generating units are estimated to be commissioned by March, 2002.

Project benefits

Besides the social and economical upliftment of the persons in its vicinity, on commissioning, NJHPP will generate 6700 million units of electrical energy in a 90% dependable year and provide 1500 MW of valuable peaking power to the Northern Grid.

Project Progress

Infrastructure work

The Excavation of all HRT Adits have been completed. Construction of the Residential Buildings as well as Non-Residential Buildings such as Administrative Office, Transit Camps, Field Hostels, Auditorium etc., have been completed.

Main civil works

The implementation of the civil works for the four major civil contracts are in progress with the three joint ventures of Indian and Foreign construction companies.

Dam complex

The slope stablisation of the right and left banks of the Dam area has been completed by installing 40/100 T cable anchors and 200 T cable anchors respectively. The slope stablisation in the Intake area is in progress with the installation of 200 T cable anchors. Out of a total number of 332 cable anchors of 200 T capacity, 193 anchors have been installed. Excavation of the dam area is undertaken for clearing of the accumulated debris during the last monsoon after the rediversion of the river in end October, 1998. So far, 11425 cum concreting has been placed in the Dam foundation area till the last working season for the placement of concreting. The excavation of the crown portion of all the four Desilting Chambers has been completed and benching down of these Chambers is in progress with steel fibre reinforced shotcrete (SFRS).

Head race tunnel

Heading excavation of a length of 26.14 km (95.4%) has been completed out of a total length of 27.39 km of HRT. Major milestones achieved were—joining up of two more Head Race Tunnel reaches -between Nathpa D/S and Sholding U/S in April, 1998, and between Sholding D/S and Nugalsari U/S in September, 1998. Benching excavation of 10.51 km of HRT has also been achieved.

Concreting of HRT from two faces and erection of Steel liners at the Manglad reach in HRT are also under progress. The 301 m. deep Surge Shaft has been fully excavated and subsequently 70% of its concreting has been achieved.

Power house complex

After the completion of excavation in the machine hall concreting of column, beam, slabs and control structure has commenced, out of which column & control structure concreting has been completed. The excavation of the Transformer Hall has also been completed and concreting of its columns & beams is in progress.

The erection of steel liners in the three Pressure Shafts is also under progress, with 52% installation having been achieved after the completion of the excavation of these pressure shafts. The concreting of the Tail Race Tunnel (TRT) has also been completed in October, 1998.

Electro-mechanical packages

The Generating Units &Associated Equipment contract was awarded to the European Consortium of M/s ABB, M/s Kvaerner Energy, Siemens, Sulzer and BHEL and became effective on November 1, 1994. Approximately, 75% of the consignment of Turbine and Generator components from the consortium agencies has been received. Two nos. EOT cranes have been commissioned in the Power House. The erection of Draft Tubes for Units I to VI has been completed. The alignment, welding & assembly of spiral casings of Units I, II & III have been completed and for Unit IV is in progress. The critical hydraulic pressure testing activity for Units I to III has also been successfully achieved. The runner alongwith shaft for the first Unit has been put in position.

Contracts have been awarded in respect of other major packages, such as (a) Butterfly Valves (b) Generator Transformers (c) GIS and Bus Ducts (d) Gates and Hoists Packages. Presently, various activities of Design and manufacturing are under progress for these packages.

Future project

NJPC is expected to take up the execution of the proposed Rampur Hydro-Electric Power Project (500600 MW), utilising the tail race waters of NJHPP as a run of the river scheme, during the IXth Plan.

Damodar Valley Corporation (DVC)

Organisation and objectives

The Damodar Valley Corporation (DVC), established on 7th July 1948 by the Damodar Valley Corporation Act, is celebrating 50th year of its service. The Corporation has a full time Chairman and two part time Members. The part time Members represent the States of Bihar and West Bengal.

The objectives of the Corporation include:

— Flood Control

— Irrigation and water supply for industrial and domestic use

— Generation, transmission and distribution of electrical energy

— Promotion of afforestation and control of soil erosion in the Damodar Valley; and

— Promotion of industrial, economic and general well-being of the people in the Damodar Valley and its areas of operation.

DVC's command area extends over an area of 24,235 sq.kms. comprising seven districts of Bihar and five districts of West Bengal.

The Corporation has so far constructed four multipurpose dams at Tilaiya, Konar, Maithon and Panchet and an irrigation system comprising a barrage on river Damodar at Durgapur and a canal system of 2459 kms. The management of Barrage and irrigation system have, however, been transferred to Government of West Bengal in 1964.

DVC power system

DVC has also constructed five thermal power stations, three hydel power stations and one gas turbine station. The existing power plants of DVC are:

Thermal

Bokaro A	175 MW (3x45 MW) & (1x40 MW)
Bokaro B	630 MW (3X210 MW)
Chandrapura	750 MW (3x130 MW) & (3x120 MW)
Durgapur	350 MW (1x 140 MW) & (1x120 MW)

Majia TIPS	Unit I	210 MW (1X210 MW)
	Unit II	210 MW (1 x21 0 MW)
	Synchronised (coal) on 31.3.1998.	
	Unit III	210 MW (1 x21 0 MW)
	Synchronised (coal) on 17.10. 1998.	

Gas turbine

GTP, Maithon	82.2 MW (3x27.5 MW)

Hydel

Tilaiya	4 MW (2X2 MW)
Maithon	60 MW (3X20 MW)
Panchet	80 MW (2x40 MW)

DVC's transmission system runs to a total length of 5350 ckt. Kms. comprising 1152 ckt. Kms. 220 kv lines, 3146 ckt. Kms. 132 kv lines and 1052 ckt. Kms. 33 kv lines. The system is supported by 52 sub-stations. The system is also interconnected with NTPC and Chukha and operates as a constituent of interconnected grid system of EREB.

DVC has already covered around 4.65 lakh ha. of land under its soil conservation activities involving worksrelating to afforestation, treatment of agricultural upland and improvement of waste land and gullied area. Around 10,000 check dams have also been constructed for controlling run-off soil and providing minor irrigation facilities.

Overall performance and achievement

During the year (April-November 1998) DVC's system generation was 4857.76 MUs of which 4578.89 MUs was contributed by thermal station, 261.05 MUs by hydel power stations and 17.81 MUs by gas turbine. During the period DVC's turnover was around Rs.1041.48 Crore (provisional) leading to profit of around Rs.38 Crore (provisional).

	Performance Highlights (April 98 - November, 98)
System Generation (MU)	4875.76
PLF (Thermal) on installed capacity(%)	37%
Turnover (Rs. Crore)	1041.48
Profit (Rs. Crore)	38

During the year (April-November 1998) DVC has achieved a number of records in the area of power generation. These include records in

Peak Generation	1312 MWon 30.10.1998
Daily Energy Generation	27.97 MU on 13.10.1998
Monthly Energy Generation	711MUduring October, 1998.
Peak Demand Met	1363 MW on 26.9.1998.

Bermo Mines

DVC's Bermo Mines produced 210247 MT of coal during April-November, 1998.

Government of India sanctioned the project in 1986, estimated cost of which stands at Rs.1989.14 Crore (third quarter 1995 price level) including IDC of Rs.427.58 Crore and WCM of Rs.9.56 crore. This has been approved. Expenditure from 4/98 to 10/98 for the project was Rs.50.70 Crore (provisional).

Unit I of the project was declared under commercial operation on 1.12.1997 while the Unit II has been synchronised in March, 1998. Coal firing after synchronisation of Unit III was achieved on 17.10.1998 for stabilising operation.

Formation work for MGR system and Rail Linkage, super structure of rail portion alongwith track laying on road bridge across Damodar river, are completed and commercial run of railway loco for transportation of coal was started. Work on railway line linking Kalidaspur coal mines is under progress. Works related to interconnection with other DVC power plants have been completed. Apart from this, out of 429 families of homestead land evictees, 402 have been shifted to rehabilitation site and compensation payment has been made to 398 evictees. Employment has been offered to 90 land losers.

Renovation and modernisation

DVC has undertaken R&M programmes in three phases with the objective of extension of plant life of its old and ageing thermal units at Bokaro 'A', Chandrapura and Durgapur and for improvement in PLF.

Comprehensive programme for BTPS'A:,CTPS & DTPS have been formulated. Though the major part of the phase II R&M work has been completed, left over work of this phase is expected to be completed by March'99. Phase III R&M scheme has been taken up for implementation during 9th Plan period. Activities for this phase have been identified in consultation with CEA, BHEL and other firms. Total estimated expenditure for the identified activities is assessed at Rs. 129.76 crore.

Renovation and Augmentation of T&D system is continuing in the 9th Plan period alongwith additional items of T&D work.

Future projects

Maithon Right Bank TPS (4x250 MW): According to the Revised Project Report for this (4x250 MW) Thermal Power Station, estimated cost of the project will be Rs.3255.20 Crore (based on 1st quarter of 1997-98 price level) without IDC. Techno-economic clearance is yet to be obtained.

Government of India have approved the proposal to implement the project as export-oriented one, through a Joint Venture Company in which DVC and BSES will have equal shareholding (45% each, the balance 10% with Financial Institutions). The two participating state governments have been asked to formally concur in.

Powergrid have been requested to plan for evacuation of power to Northern Region via Sasaram and to Western Region via Rourkela.

Combined cycle gas turbine

The existing 82.5 MW (3x27.5 MW) Single Cycle Gas Turbine Station at Maithon has been planned to be converted to combined cycle which would add 45 MW (3x15 MW) extra to the station. Estimated cost is likely to be around Rs. 150 Crore and funding arrangement is yet to be identified.

Bhakra Beas Management Board (BBMS)

Bhakra Management Board (BMB) was constituted under section 79 of the Punjab Re-organisation Act, 1966 for the administration, maintenance and operation of Bhakra Nangal Project w.e.f 1st October, 1967. The Beas Project works, on completion, were transferred by the Government of India from Beas Construction Board (BCB) to BMB as per Section 80 of the Act, 1966 and the Bhakra Management Board was renamed as Bhakra Beas Management Board (BBMB) w.e.f 15.5.1976.

Functions

The Bhakra Beas Management Board manages the facilities created for harnessing the waters impounded at Bhakra and Pong in addition to those diverted at Pandoh through the BSL Water Conductor System. It was also assigned the responsibility of delivering water and power to the beneficiary States in accordance with their due/entitled shares. The Board is responsible for the administration, maintenance and operation works at Bhakra Nangal Project, Beas Project Unit I and Unit II including Power Houses and a network of transmission lines and grid sub-stations. The functions of Bhakra Beas Management Board are:

To regulate the supply of Sutlej and Ravi-Beas waters to the States of the Punjab, Haryana, Rajasthan and Delhi, through a wide network of canals.

To distribute power from Bhakra Nangal and Beas projects to the States of Punjab, Haryana, Rajasthan, Himachal Pradesh and U.T. of Chandigarh.

The works being managed by the BBMB are broadly grouped as three large multipupose projects viz. Bhakra Nangal Project, Beas Project Unit-I (BSL Project) and Beas Project Unit-II (Pong Dam).

The Bhakra Nangal Project comprises the Bhakra Dam, Bhakra Left Bank and Bhakra Right Bank Power Houses, Nangal Dam, Nangal Hydel Channel and Ganguwal and Kotla Power Houses. Bhakra Dam is a majestic monument across the river Sutlej. It is a high straight gravity concrete Dam rising 225.55 m (740 ft.) above the deepest foundation and spanning the gorge with 518.16 m (1700 ft.) length at the top. The Gobind Sagar lake created by the Dam has 168.35 Sq.Km. area and a gross storage capacity of 9651 million cubic-metre (7.80 MAF). The two power houses, one on the Left Bank (5x108=540 MW) and the other on the Right Bank (2xl 32+3xl 57=735 MW) , have a combined installed capacity of 1275 MW. The Ganguwal and Kotla Power Houses fed from Nangal Hydel Channel have an installed capacity of 162.65 MW.

The Beas Project Unit-I (BSL Project) diverts Beas Water into the Sutlej Basin, failing from a height of 320 metre (1050 ft.) and generating power at Dehar power House having an installed capacity of 6x165 MW = 990 MW. This Project comprises a diversion dam at Pandoh,

13.1 Km long Pandoh Baggi Tunnel having capacity of 9000 Cusec, 11.8 Km. long Sundernagar Hydel Channel, Balancing reservoir at Sundernagar, 12.35 Km. long Sundernagar Sutlej Tunnel, 125 Metre high Surge Shaft and Dehar Power Plant.

The Beas Dam at Pong is the highest earth fill (earth core, gravel shell) Dam in India, being 132.6 metre (435 ft.) high with a live storage capacity of 7290 million cubic metre (5.91 MAF). The Pong Power Plant (5x60+1x66=366 MW) is located in the stilling basin d/ s of penstock tunnels.

The total installed generating capacity of the BBMB Power Houses is 2793.65 MW detailed as under:

Power House	Installed Capacity
Bhakra (Right Bank)	2X 132+3X157 = 735
Bhakra (Left Bank)	5X 108 =540
Ganguwal	1X27.63+1X24.2+1X29.25= 51.57
Kotla	1X28.12+1X24.2+1X29.25 = 81.57
Dehar	6X165 = 990
Pong	5X 60+1X66 =366
Total	2793.65 MW

Generation & transmission system

The BBMB Power Plants have the highest plant availability factor (90 to 94%).

The Generation during 1997-98 was 10686 MU. The generation during the year 1998-99 is expected to be about 13650 MU against the target of 10650 MU (about 28% more) which will be the maximum recorded generation since the construction of Bhakra Nangal Project and Beas Project (Unit-I and Unit-II).

The power generation at BBMB power stations is

being evacuated through BBIVIB power evacuation system running into 3775 circuit Km length of 400 KV, 220 KV, 132 KV and 66 KV transmission lines and 24 EHV substations. The BBIVIB power evacuation system operates in an integrated manner in the Northern grid with its transmission network spreading over the States of Himachal Pradesh, Punjab, Haryana and Delhi. The system is interconnected with transmission system of Power Grid and the States of Uttar Pradesh, Rajasthan and Delhi.

Renovation and modernisation

All the 5 units of Bhakra Right Bank Power Houses are being uprated from original capacity of 120 MW to 157 MW each. This will result in gain of installed capacity by 185 MW and an additional annual energy generation of 310 MUs. Uprating of Unit No.9, Unit No.6 and Unit No.8 has been completed in February 1996, June 1997 and April, 1998 respectively.

The R&M and uprating of Ganguwal and Kotla Power Houses has been planned in two phases. In phase 1, the R&M and Uprating of one Unit each at Ganguwal and Kotla Power Houses had been approved. The Unit No.2 at Ganguwal Power House after R&M and uprating from 24.2 MW to 27.63 MW was commissioned on 4.1.1998 while the R&M and uprating of Unit No.3 at Kotla Power House from 24.2 MW to 28.12 MW was completed on 1.10.1998.

This has resulted in the enhancement in the installed capacity of these two units by 7.35 MW and an additional annual generation of 63 MUs. In Phase-II, the R&M and uprating of one more unit each at Ganguwal and Kotla Power Houses is under process. This will result in capacity enhancement of 5.94 MW and an increased annual generation of 49 MUs.

Uprating and Modernisation of one unit of Pong Power Plant from 60 MW to 66 MW has been completed on 23.2.1998. Uprating and Modernisation of the remaining units will also be taken up. The benefits include additional peaking capacity of 36 MW, additional annual generation of 173 LUs in good monsoons when spillage becomes inevitable, apart from the additional 90 MVAR reactive power and life extension of the units.

Central Power Research Institute (CPRI)

The Central Power Research Institute (CPRI) was established in Bangalore by the Government of India in 1960. It was organised into an autonomous society in the year 1978 under the aegis of the Ministry of Power, Government of India. The main objective of setting up the Institute was to serve as a National Laboratory for undertaking applied research in electric power engineering besides functioning as an independent National Testing and Certification Authority for electrical equipment and components to ensure reliability and improve, innovate and develop new products. More specifically the objectives cover the following:

Objectives

— To serve as a national centre for applied research in electrical power engineering.

— To function as an independent and impartial authority for testing & certification of electrical equipments manufactured in the country for quality assurance.

— Performing tests for product development.

— To offer consultancy on problems referred to by utilities and industries.

— Undertake sponsored research programmes on subjects of interest in the power system field.

The institute is headed by a Director General and has several research laboratories and testing facilities, and employ about 280 qualified scientists and engineers besides other supporting staff guiding and maintaining various operations. The Head Office of the Institute is at Bangalore and its other units are located at Bhopal, Hyderabad, Nagpur, Ghaziabad, Thiruvananthapuram and Raichur.

Performance and achievements at a glance

The CPRI continued to play a vital role in quality assurance to ensure reliability of power equipment through testing and certification in accordance with national and international standards. The institute has been meeting its non-plan expenditure through revenue generated by testing and consultancy for the last ten years and the revenue has been increasing over the years. The trend is expected to continue also during the current year.

The institute recorded a revenue of Rs. 1256.12 lakh upto November 1998 which is 2% more than that of the previous year and it is expected to reach the target of Rs. 2300 lakh by the year end. Marketing & Publicity has been given a boost by participating in International exhibitions. This has resulted in an increase in the testing orders by foreign clients. The total foreign exchange earnings estimated for the year 1998-99 is Rs.50 lakh and the earnings were $ 57000/ - upto 30th November, 1998 as compared to UA $ 16000/ earned during the previous year ending march, 1998.

With a goal to achieving full automation in all the activities through computerisation and also mechanisation of testing activity for speedy preparation of test reports several servers have been added for fast communication. Test report generation is automated in Short Circuit laboratory and similar work will be completed in three more laboratories viz., High Voltage and High power Laboratories of Bangalore and STDS Bhopal. To keep abreast with the latest information technology and global communication the internet communication over leased line was established and is available on the Local Area campus wide Network.

New test facilities

Some of the new test facilities added during the year are:

— D.C. Test facility for testing LV Switchgear & Controlgear etc. as per International & Indian standards.

— EMI/EMC test facility at both Bangalore & Bhopal units.

— Reference voltage divider for calibration of voltage divider used for measuring AC, DC and lightning/ switching impulse voltages.

— Dynamic performance characteristic test of impedance relay.

— High current unit source for testing OCR relays.

— High current test facility for testing switchgear upto 300 kA rms for 1.0 sec/3 phase.

— Endurance test on full size power capacitors.

— Charge & discharge cycle test on self healing type capacitors.

— High Voltage withstand test on surge protection capacitors.

Unique tests carried out in CPRI

— Short Circuit current test at 8 kA for 3 seconds was conducted on the tap changers as per IEC 214-1989.

— 300 HP, 3 phase induction motor was tested at the IP

& Rotating Machines Laboratory for the first time as per IS 4691 - 1985.

— Lightning impulse test on 20 MVA, 66/11 kV 3 phase transformer on both HV & LV windidngs 8 kV, 220 KV capacitor as per IS 2834 —1986 with latest amendments.

— Surge arrester leakage rate test as per Australian standard 1037-2 (1987) for the first time in the country.

— Partial Discharge test on 630 kVA & 1000 kVA, 11 kV/433 Resin cast Distribution transformer using double frequency source for the first time.

— DC test on earthing switch as per IEC 77 for the first time.

CPRI has taken a giant step in giving engineering support to utilities. In consortium with M/s. Black & Vetch India Ltd., the Institute has been registered by PFC (Power Finance Corporation) as a qualified consultant for taking up repair, maintenance, life evaluation and extension studies in coal based Thermal Power Stations in India. The Institute has bagged a ranking of BB+ by Power Finance Corporation amongst shortlisted vendors. With this, it is expected that the Institute will engage itself as a major consultant in the area of Thermal Power Engineering.

The Institute continued its strides in the area of research by successfully competing seven projects upto November end out of a total of 80 ongoing and new projects. Notable achievements include development of low inductance resistance divider for measurement of steep front impulse voltage, evaluation of treeing phenomenon in XLPE Cables, study of Design of harmonic filters for distribution system, low cost single phase tamper proof energy meter (0.2 class), development of condensate depression monitor for TPS, development of arc heater for simulation and testing arcing in high enthalpy gas flows etc. A new thrust is given to orient the research towards the benefit of the power utilities and the manufacturing industries. This resulted in stepping up of liaison with the utilities, industries and academic institutions for promoting joint research projects. As an off shoot of R&D efforts, several patents were filed. The patents obtained & sealed by the institute are given below:

Patent obtained

During the year the Institute obtained the following patent for the invention relating to:

— Development of New Aluminium Conductors for Coastal applications.

— Fluidised bed updraft multifuel biomass gasifiers.

Patent sealed

— Development of spherical electrode digital field meter.

— Hand held battery operated capacitance detector.

— Zirconium based ceramic powder for plasma spray.

— Development of metal chellates for faster curing of Epoxy resin system

Collaborative activities with industry

CPRI continued its course of collaboration with other organisations by signing Memoranda of Understanding and for commercialisation of the technologies already developed. They are:

— M/s. Poet Consultants Pvt. Ltd. And M/s Black & Vetch India Ltd. for undertaking Retro, fitting and modernisation, remaining life assessment/life extention studies on Coal fired Thermal Power stations in the country.

- Kerala State Women Development Corporation, transfer of technology on Electronic Ballast developed by CPRI.
- CPRI and NTPC for joint studies and developing facilities and expertise in the areas of common interest.

— M/s. FARCOM Cable Systems Pvt. Ltd. for joint development of FRLS cable insulation and sheathing materials under DST-DSIR (PATSER) scheme and for upscaling the project to pilot plant scale for Indian Cable Industries on a long term basis.

— ANERT (Agency for Non-Conventional Energy & Rural Technology, Thiruvananthapuram for development of Stirling Engine run by Biomoss gasifier and installation, commissioning of the engine at a site identified by ANERT for field demonstration.

— EDF, France for developmental studies of common interest in the field of High Power Current testing & measuring devices and for complementary testing between the two laboratories.

Technical consultancy

Consultancy to M/s. Power Grid Corporation of India Ltd. for long term measurement of harmonic levels at their 1500 MW, 500 kV bipole of HVDC substation at Rihand. These measurements are required for the assessment of the performance of the Rihand-Dadri 500 kV bipole of HVDC line with an approximate transmission length around 1000 km.

Consultancy services were provided to High Power Committee appointed by the Supreme Court to study the existing metering system for Electricity in Uttar Pradesh

State Electricity Board and recommended measures to minimise theft of electricity.

During the year, 18 technical reports were brought out covering the outcome of research in various areas and a large number of technical papers were presented in both National and Internation seminars/workshops.

Two IX Plan capital projects involving a total outlay of Rs.876.88 lakh are under various stages of implementation.

National Power Training Institute (NPTI)

National Power Training Institute (NPTI) has been set up by Government of India to function as the National Apex Body for the Human Resources Development of Power Sector personnel in India.

The Headquarters of NPTI is located at NPTI Complex, Sector - 33, Faridabad (Haryana). It operates on all India basis through its four Regional Power Training Institutes located at Neyveli (Tamil Nadu), Durgapur (West Bengal), Badarpur (New Delhi) and Nagpur (Maharashtra). The NPTI including its four Regional Power-Training Institutes, is fully equipped with the latest state-of-the-art training infrastructure and having expert faculties with long years of professional and teaching background.

The Institutes are conducting a number of training programmes for Power Engineers, Operators and Technicians in the areas of Thermal and Hydro Power Generation, Power System and other related areas. The Training Institute at Badarpur is equipped with a computer based full scope replica simulator of 210 MW Fossil Fuel Thermal Power Plant to provide off-job/ hands on training.

Two more simulators of 500 MW and 210 MW have

been commissioned at NPTI HQ., Faridabad and at Nagpur Institute respectively. In addition, an Institute for Advanced Learning & Management Studies for higher echelons of Power Sector is being established at NPTI Complex, Faridabad. It will have departments in specialised areas of Hydro, Thermal, Power System and Management Studies.

It will function as a nodal Institute for Power Sector training not only for designing, implementing and supervising the whole power sector training activities but also to create the right type of organisational culture.

Activities/achievement training output

Upto November, 1998, 46144 personnel of various level from different Organisation have been trained at the four Training Institutes of NPTI since their inception. 4500 personnel have been trained on the 210 MW simulator at Badarpur Institute since its installation. NPTI has trained 1078 trainees at its four Regional Power Training Institutes upto November, 1998. 178 personnel have been trained on the newly commissioned 210 MW Simulator at RPTI, Nagpur during this period. NPTI has achieved 10635 trainees weeks upto Nov'98 against the yearly target of 22959 trainee weeks.

Post graduate diploma in thermal power plant engineering

NPTI also conducts one year Post Graduate Diploma Course in Thermal Power Plant Engineering since 1996 for fresh and experienced engineers. 135 engineers are currently undergoing training under this programme. The fourth batch of the Post Graduate Diploma Course in Thermal Power Plant Engineering will commence in August, 1999.

Specialised training programmes

— One day workshops on Energy Efficiency Management in Thermal Power Stations and Electricity Accounting System was organised at NPTI HQ, Faridabad on 10th July, 1998 and 18th September, 1998 respectively. The workshops were sponsored by M/s Power Finance Corporation. About 50 senior level Executives from various Power Sector organisations attended each workshop.

— A one day seminar on World Environment Day was organised on 5.6.1998 at RPTI, Durgapur in association with Institution of Engineers, Durgapur Chapter and Pollution Control Board. 71 persons attended the seminar.

— A two week specialised programme on Power Plant Operation was organised for Engineers/ Operating staff of NTPC, NCPP, Dadri at RPTI, Badarpur.

— A five week on-site training programme for Engineers of Guru Hargovind Thermal Power Plant, Bhatinda was conducted. The programme covered Power Plant Familiarisation, Scheme Tracing and Operating aspects.

— A ten week specialised training programme on Information Technology for senior Supervisors of NHPC was organised at RPTI, Badarpur.

— A one week on site training programme on "Power System and Energy Losses" was conducted at Technical training Centre, Electricity Deptt. Pondicherry by RPTI Neyveli.

— A three day on site training Programme on Boiler Operation was conducted at FACAT Management Development Centre Kalamasery Cochin for the serving personnel of Fertiliser and Chemicals Travancore Limited by RPTI Neyveli.

Computer based training

Facilities for Computer Based Training (CBT) has been

fully established with the assistance of ODA, UK. A CBT Cell has been set up at NPTI Head quarters for developing the CBT (self-learning) packages on various technical areas concerning power generation.

A number of multimedia CBT packages on different topics have since been developed and available for use by Power Sector Companies at their Training Centres. This Cell also provides assistance to the SEBs and Utilities in establishing self-learning centres aided by CBT packages in their respective organisations. Nuclear Power Corporation is already making use of these packages-

Consultancy services

NPTI has diversified into different areas of consultancy such as setting up of training institutes, assessment of training needs, recruitment etc.

Implementation of on-going schemes

The following Schemes are under implementation:

— Setting up of Institute for Advanced Learning & Management Studies at NPTI Headquarters.

— Installation of 210 MW Simulator at RPTI, Nagpur.

— Installation of 500 MW Simulator at Faridabad.

— Computer Based Training.

— Renovation & Modernisation of existing 210 MW Simulator at RPTI, Badarpur.

New schemes Management Centre (EMC)

The following New Schemes have been proposed during the Ninth Plan:

— Augmentation of Regional Power training Institutes.

— Setting up of Training Institute in North Eastern Region.

— Setting up of Environmental Cell/Augmentation of NPTI.

— Setting up of Training Institute for Hydro Power.

— Augmentation of CBT Scheme.

— Expenditure on Training at NPTI/RPTIs to be treated as Plan.

These schemes have been accepted in principle for a total outlay of Rs. 117.05 Crore.

Energy Management Centre (EMC)

Energy management Centre was set up in April, 1989 as an autonomous organisation under Ministry of Power and in collaboration with European Community to strengthen the energy management capabilities in the country. It serves as a executive agency of Ministry of Power. It has been focusing its attention on research, training of senior technical personnel and development of data on energy usage and dissemination of information to the main energy consuming sectors through workshop, seminars, multimedia, awareness campaign etc.

EMC also helps in formulation of policy and designing of programme on energy conservation and serves as a nodal point at the central level for monitoring and co ordinating of energy; conservation activities in the country. A sum of Rs.25 lakhs was provided in the Central annual budget as grant-in-aid to EMC for the year 1998-99.Activities undertaken/completed by EMC during the year 1998-99 include the following:

— DSM Plan for Gujrat Electricity Board.

— Energy Saving in Aluminium Electrolysis by bringing down the operating temperature of Electrolyte.

— Manual on Energy Efficiency in Pumping System.

— Projects on Energy Efficient Motors, Variable Speed Drives and Air Compression System.

International programme

— India EC Energy Management Co-operation Programme.

— Indo GTZ Programme.

— Energy Efficiency Support Project of ADB.

— India-Us Energy efficiency Cooperation Programme.

— World Bank Project on India regarding environmental issues in the power sector.

Dissemination of information was carried out through sale/distribution of EMC publication and display and sale of video cassettes on energy conservation.

11

Other Important Activities

Consultative committee of members of parliament

During the year 1998-99 the Ministry of Power coordinated and organized three meetings of the Consultative Committee of Members of Parliament for the Ministry of Power. The subjects for discussion at these meetings were (1) Power Grid Corporation of India Ltd; (ii) Power Scenario in the Country; and (iii) Hydro Power Policy.

Implementation of official language policy

The Ministry of Power, its attached and subordinate offices and public sector undertakings/Autonomous Bodies/Boards/Societies/Institutions under the administrative control of Ministry of Power have continued their efforts in ensuring effective implementation of the official language policy of the Government and encouraging progressively the use of Hindi in official work.

In compliance with the constitutional and statutory requirements of Section 3(3) of Official Language Act as amended from time to time, all documents required to be issued bilingually are being issued bilingually by the Ministry. Similarly all communications received in Hindi are replied to in Hindi compulsorily. The Subcommittee of Parliament on Official Language visited Ministry of Power on 4.1.99 and Committee appreciated the performance of Ministry of Power in the field of Official language.

Hindi Salahkar Samiti of the Ministry of Power has been reconstituted on 21.12.98 Meeting of Official Language Implementation Committee of the Ministry of Power were also regularly convened during the year 1998-99. Cash award schemes such as Incentive Scheme for Original Noting/Drafting in Hindi as well as Hindi Dicatation Scheme formulated and circulated by the Deptt. Of Official Language, Ministry of Home Affairs for promoting the use of Hindi in official work continued to be followed in the Ministry, its attached offices.

With a view to assessing the progressive use of Hindi in various offices of undertakings/Autonomous bodies/Boards/Institutions under the administrative control of Ministry, periodic inspections were made.

In compliance with the official language policy, a "Hindi Pakhwara" were celebrated in the Ministry of Power from 1.9.1998 to 15.9.1998 to step up the use of Hindi in official work. Competitions in Hindi essay writing, Hindi debate, Hindi poetry and Hindi typing were organised. Officers/employees of the Ministry took part in the competitions.

To encourage the progressive use of Hindi through positive competitiveness among the attached and subordinatge offices and Public Sector Undertakings/ Autonomous Bodies/Boards/Societies/institutions under the administrative control of Ministry of Power, a scheme for awarding Vidyut Rajbhasha Running Shield, Rajbhasha Trophy and Rajbhasha cup was introduced and the successful participants such as NTPC, New Delhi, CPRI, Bangalore, Power Grid, New Delhi, BBMB, Chandigarh, THDC, New Delhi, NEEPCO, Shillong were awarded Vidyut Rajbhasha Shield, Vidyut Rajbhasha Trophy and Vidyut Rajbhasha Cup respectively for their excellent performance in the field of official Language Policy.

Vigilance activities disciplinary cases

At the begining of the year 1998-99, there were eleven disciplinary cases pending with the Ministry. Two new cases were initiated. Out of these thirteen cases, seven cases have been disposed off during the year. The remaining six cases are at various stages of processing. Proposals for initiation of disciplinary proceedings in three more cases were under examination at the end of January, 1999.

Welfare of minorities

The Prime Minister's 15 point programme on Welfare of Minorities is being implemented in the Ministry of Power. It has been ensured that in case of direct recruitment to Group 'C' and 'D' posts, a member of minority community is included in the selection committee.

SC/ST Cell is functioning under the control of the Liaison Office who is of the rank of Deputy Secretary. The function of the SC/ST Cell is to assist the Liaison Officer in monitoring implementation of the reservation policies of the Government in all the Public Sector Undertakings under the administrative control of the Ministry including autonomous bodies and attached offices. SC/ST Cell also sends periodical reports viz., consolidated annual statements to Department of Personnel and Training and Department of Public Enterprises.

It also helps the Liaison Office in his annual inspection of the rosters maintained by various organisations of the Ministry. It also deals with the grievances cases of SC/ST officials of various organisations under the Ministry. In 1998, the cell has received 24 grievances from SC/ST officials and has redressed 18 grievances till date. The remaining 6 grievances are under process and will be disposed off soon. SC/ST cell also assists the Liaison Officer (OBC) in monitoring implementation of OBC reservation in all the organisations under the administrative control.

Grievances cell

The Grievances Cell of Ministry of Power dealt with 38 cases relating to various grievances pertaining to pension, pensionary benefits, transfer, pay fixation, seniority, employment on compassionate grounds etc. Out of 38 cases, 18 cases have been disposed off. Grievance Redressal Machinery of PFC was inspected on 22nd September, 1998. The programme to inspect other Public Sector Undertakings under the control of the Ministry of power is under process.

Controller of accounts

The Office of the Controller of Accounts has four Pay & Accounts Offices working under his payment control, viz; PAO, CEA, New Delhi; PAO(CEA), Bangalore; PAO (Sectt.), New Delhi and PAO (BMCC), New Delhi. The monthly accounts of these offices are submitted regularly to the Principal Accounts Office. Thereafter these are consolidated and sent to the Off ice of the Controller General of Accounts, Ministry of Finance in a detailed classified form.

The payment on account of DCRG, Pension, commuted value of pension and GPF to the officials (of the Ministry of Power/Central Electricity Authority) on retirement during the year were made in time.

The Principal Accounts Office is also responsible for the preparation of Appropriation Accounts, Statement of Central Transactions (SCT) and Finance Account on annual basis for submission to the Controller General of accounts (CGA).

The Principle Accounts Office also brought out the document 'Accounts at a Glance' for 1997-98. The office of the COA is fully responsible for preparing the Receipt Budget of the Ministry.

Computerisation of accounts

The office of the Controller of Accounts utilises the software packages integrated moduler for processing voucher (improve) and controller's accounting (contract) provided by the CGA. The voucher level computerisation has been carried out in all the four PAOs. The consolidation of monthly accounts of all the PAOs in Ministry of Power is done by using the contact software package. Various other packages like SCT are also used for report Generation. Reports are also generated from the options provided in Report Generation Menu in contact.

The accounts consolidated through the contact programme are then sent by the Controller of accounts to the Controller General of Accounts (CGA) for the preparation of Finance Account and the Appropriation Accounts of the Government of India.

Internal audit wing

The internal Audit Wing ensures adoption of sound procedure, regularities and financial propriety of transactions and accounts. This Wing advises the DDOs and their staff for correct implementation of rules and maintenance of proper records. Internal Audit wing also pursues the settlement of objections raised by the Statutory Audit.

The organisation-wise break-up of Audit observations and Inspection Reports as on 31.3.1998 are as under:

Audit observation

The organisation-wise back-up of Audit observations and inspection reports as on 31.3. 1998 are as to the next page:

Audit objections on 31.3. 1998

Organisation	No.of Inspection Reports	No. of Paras
1 . Ministry of Power	5	29
2. Central Electricity Authority	1	29
Pay & Accounts office/controller of accounts		
3. PAO(CEA), New Delhi	8	21
4. PAO (BMCC), New Delhi	1	4
5. PAO (Sectt.), New Delhi	3	10
6. PAO(CEA), Bangalore	1	6
Total	19	99

Recreation activities

The Ministry is promoting sports and cultural activities. Power Sports Control Board (PSCB), with the Minister in-charge of the Ministry of Power as Chairman, constituted as a nodal agency with the participation of Central Power Organisation i e. Central Electricity Authority and all the Public Sector Undertakings/ Autonomous bodies etc. under the administrative control of the Ministry of Power, is arranging various tournaments in various disciplines every year, all over the country with the help of member organisations.

The Board got formally registered as a society under the Societies Regulation Act, 1860 on May 13, 1994. The Ministry is encouraging the participation of its officers and staff in several sports and cultural meets.

The Ministry has a Recreation Club for its staff for looking after the cultural and sports activities. The Hon'ble Minister of Power and the Secretary (P) are its Chief patron and patron, respectively.

12

Industry and Power Sectors

As a result of sound policies pursued over the years, tremendous development has taken place in India industry, which stands today on a sound footing. However, there are certain infrastructural weaknesses which need to be tackled to ensure further growth. Indian industry has undergone a sea change since Independence. From a situation, where even a pin had to be inported, India has reached a stage when it is going to manufacture 50-seater and 100-seater passenger aircraft. What is more, the Indian consumer today has a wide variety of goods to choose from. The Indian market place is today loaded with a range of goods. Whether it is newer models of cars, scooters or mlobikes, washing machines, sooking range or mixies there ia large variety to choose from. Gone are the days when choices were limited and one had to wait almost a year to get delivery of a new car or a scooter. One can today walk into a show room and drive out. With a choice available to the consumer the quality of goods have also shown distinct improvement.

Indian industry at the time of Independence was at a rudimentary stage. It was confined to cotton and jute textiles, which accounted for 56.8 per cent of value-added in manufacturing sugar (6.6 per cent), engineering (8.4 per cent), steel (7.6 per cent), chemicals (4.1 per cent) and cement (2.1 per cent). Modern industry formed only six to eight per cent of national income in Independence India in 1950, with small scale enterprises and mining contributing 12 to 14 per cent. A feature of India's industrial sector soon after Independence was the virtual absence of capital or producers goods industry. Indian industries had to rely almost wholly on imported machinery and machine tools. In 1950, India met 89.8 per cent of its need for machine tools through imports, producing internally only Rs. 30 lakh worth of machine tools and portable tools.

The foundations of modern India's industrial economy was laid by Jawaharlal Nehru, who led the country to freedom and thereafter as Prime Minister for nearly 17 years, built the country's economy form a scratch. This was done through the public sector, whose foundations were laid by Nehru, as the private sector did not have the resources to undertake huge infrastructure projects, like Bhakra hydro-electric power project, or steel plants like Bhilai, whom the great visionary described as the temples of modern India Nehru realised that without the basic infrastructure industries, the foundations of a modern industrial economy could not be laid. If this war true in 1950, it is equally true today as infrastructural bottlenecks are constraining growth.

Industrial growth after Independence was facilitated by the Industrial Policy Resolution of 1948, followed by the Industrial Policy Resolution of 1956, which had as its objective, the acceleration of the rate of economic growth and the speeding up of industrialisation as a means of achieving a socialist pattern of Society. In 1956 capital was scarce and the base of entrepreneurship was not strong enough. Hence the 1956 Industrial Policy Resolution, gave primacy to the role of the state to assume predominant and direct responsibility for industrial development. Special importance was given in the two resolutions of 1948 and 1956 to the development of steel, heavy engineering, machine tools and heavy chemicals industry.

The industrial policy resolution of 1948 has a small number of industries to be reserved for production by the public sector. These included the production and control of atomic energy and ownership and managment of railways. However, coal, iron and steel, aircraft manufacturing, shipbuilding, manufacture of telegraph and wireless equipment (except radios) and minerals were reserved for production by Central or State government undertakings. The 1956 industrial Policy Resolution added some more industries to the list. The original thinking was that as far as the public sector was concerned, it should enter fields where private sector would find it difficult to invest. By 1956, this had changed to an absolute preference for state ownership of industries and the public sector was supposed to capture the commanding heights of the economy.

Since Independence, the public sector in India has been guided by the Industrial Policy Resolution of 1956, which had as its objectives the acceleration of the rate of economic growth and speeding up of the industrialisation as means of achieving the socialistic pattern of society. Since in the initial phase of industrialisation, the capital was scare, the state sector assumed the predominance and direct responsibility for industrial development. The size of public sector in India is indeed very large. It includes government departments and its compaines whether in the Central or state sector, irrigation and power projects, railways, posts and telegraphs, ordnance factories and other departmental undertakings, banking, insurance, financial and other services. The focus here is however, on the Central public sector enterprises established as Government companies or statutory corporations excluding banking units.

After the initial exuberance of public sector entering into new areas of industrial manufacturing, providing technical services, trading, financial and services sectors, the public enterprises started facing various problems, some of these problems were due to historical reasons, while others were related to poor project management, over-manning, obsolete technology, poor order book positions etc. All these put together, the public sector as a whole started showing results far below the desired level in comparison to the investments made in them.

The Government announced a new Industrial Policy on 24 July 1991 which envisages liberalisation, competitive environment. The new Policy has laid down certain specific areas in respect of the public enterprises which are to be emphasized in order to make them better performers and more competitive. The slient features of the new Industrial Policy on the Public Sector are: (i) Portfolio of public sector investments will be reviewed with a veiw to focus the public sector on strategic, high-tech and essential infrastructure. Whereas some reservation for the public sector is being retained, there would be no bar for area exclusively to be opened up to the private sector selectively. Similarly, the public sector will also be allowed entry in areas not reserved for it; (ii) Public enterprises which are chronically sick and which are unlikely to be turned around will for the formulation of revival, rehabilitation schemes, be referred to the Board for Industrial and Financial Reconstruction (BIFR), or other similar high level institutions created for the purpose. A social security mechanism will be created to protect the interest of workers likely to be affected by such rehabilitation packages; (iii) in order to raise resources and encourage wider public participation, a part of the governement's share-holding in the public sector would be offered to mutual funds, financial institutions, general public and workers; (iv) Boards of public sector companies would be made more professional and given greater powers; (v) there will be a greater thrust on performance improvement through the Memoranda of Understanding (MOU) system through which management would be granted greater autonomy and will be held accountable. Technical expertise on the part of the Goernment would be upgraded to make the MOU negotiations and implementation more effective; and (vi) to facilitate a fuller discussion on performance, the MOU singed between Government and the public enterprise would be placed in Parliament. While focussing on major management issues, this would also help place matters on day to day operations of public enterprises in their perspective.

As a major step for implementation of the Policy, the Government of India has disinvested varying percentage of its share-holdings in some PSUs. So far, the shares of 39 PSUs, have been disinvested in favour of the financial institutions, mutual funds, banks, foreign institutional investors and the public. This resulted in disinvestment of 152.07 crore share in 39 public sector undertakings and a sum of Rs. 9,794 crore was realised.

The shares of these companies are now listed on the stock exchanges. The valuation of the equity of these enterprises on the stock exchanges reflects the preceptions of the public in general and investors in particular of the performance and the expectations of the public from these enterprises. Besides, the Government has also offered a part of its equity holdings in some of these enterprises in favour of the employees, in order to encourage the employees participation in the managements a sence of commitment and belonging to an enterprise.

Over a period of time, the public enterprises have been faced with the chronical sickness and mounting losses. In the case of some of the enterprises, which have incurred huge losses and had eroded their networth, in order to formulate the revival/rehabilitation packages, a number of these enterprises have been referred to the Board for Industrial and Financial Reconstruction (BIFR). So far, 54 sick enterprises have been referred to BIFR for revival/rehabilitation. BIFR makes an independent assessment of the viability or otherwise of a particular enterprise afte keeping in the view points of the owner (Government), the employees, the financial institutions and the other concerned. Under the new Industrial Policy, greater thrust has been laid on the evaluation of the performance, through the system of MOUs which has also started yielding positive results in the form of better performance from the public enterprises.

There has been appreciable growth in the investments in the public sector over the years. In 1951, the investment in five Central Public Sector was Rs. 29 crore. This investment has gone up to Rs. 147,587 crore in 245 enterprises as on 31 March 1993 and at Rs. 164,332 crore in 246 enterprises in 1993-94. Thus, during 1993-94, the investment in public sector has increased by Rs. 16,745 crore registering an increase of 11.35 per cent.

Public sector has been playing a dominant role in the fertilizer industry. The first state-owned fertilizer unit was set up in 1951 at Sindri in Bihar, which was followed by another plant at Nangal in Punjab. With the coming up of another fertilizer plant at Trombay, Government decided to bring all the public sector fertilizer units under the management of a single undertaking and the Fertilizer Corporation of India Limited (FCI) was accordingly incorporated in January 1961. The National Fertilizers Limited was established on 23 August 1974.

Thereafter, the Fertilizer Corporation of India and the National Fertilizers Limited were re-organised into four companies on the basis of feedstock used and geographical considerations from 1 April 1978. At present, there are nine public sector undertakings under the administrative control of Department of Fertilizers. FCI has now four units, one each at Sindri (Bihar), Gorakhpur (U.P.) Talcher (Orissa) and Ramagundam (Andhra Pradesh), with a total installed capacity of 5.87 lakh tonnes of nitrogen.

The National Fertilizers Limited (NFL) has, at present, five operating units, *viz.*, the calcium ammonium nitrate plant at Nanagal and the urea plants at Nanagal, Bhatinda, Panipat and Vijaipur. With the commissioning of the Vijaipur plant in 1987-88, the total installed capacity of NFL has gone up to 10.36 lakh MT· of nitrogen, making NFL the largest producer of nitrogenous fertilizers in the country.

The Fertilizers and Chemicals Travancore Limited (FACT), Udyogamandal (Kerala), has, at present, three operating units, one at Udyogamandal and two at Cochin. Besides fertilizers, the company is engaged in the manufacture of chemicals. With the commissioning of caprolactum plant in October 1990, the company has entered the field of petro-chemicals also. FACT Engineering and Design Organisation (FEDO), another division of the company is engaged in design, engineering, procurement, supervision of construction and commissioning of fertilizers/chemical plants.

Rashtriya Chemicals and Fertilizers Limited (RCF) is in charge of the Trombay plants and the large gas-based fertilizer plant at Thal which started commercial production in 1985. Hindustan Fertilizer Corporation Limited has five units in production, three at Namrup in Assam and one each at Durgapur in West Bengal and

Barauni in Bihar, having total annual installed capacity of 6.54 lakh tonnes of nitrogen. Madras Fertilizers Limited (MFL) is a joint venture, with the Government of India holding 67.55 per cent of the equity share capital and the National Iranian Oil Company holding the remaining 32.45 per cent.

The annual installed capacity of MFL is 1.76 lakh tonnes of nitrogen and 1.12 lakh tonnes of phosphate. Pyrites, Phosphates and Chemicals Limited (PPCL), set up in March 1960, is presently engaged in the exploration of pyrites deposits as well as production of single super phosphate at Amjhore in Bihar, exploration-cumproduction mining of pyrites deposits at Saladipura in Rajasthan and mining of rock phosphate ore from the Mussuoorie phosphorite deposits

Projects and Development India Limited (PDIL), formerly known as Fertilizer (Planning & Development) India Limited, is engaged in design, engineering, procurement and supervision of construction/ commissioning of fertilizer and allied chemical plants. The company has played a pioneering role in developing, entirely on its own initiative, the know-how for manufacture of catalysts in India. Pradeep Phosphates L:imited (PPL) was established in December, 1981 for setting up a phosphatic fertilizer complex at Paradeep in Orissa. Phase-I of the project, comprising 7.20 lakh TAP capacity DAP plant and allied facilities was commissioned in 1986. Phase-II of the project, comprising sulphuric acid and phosphoric acid plants, also went into commercial production in June 1992.

Indian Farmers Fertilizer Cooperative Limited (IFFCO) incrporated in 1975 and Krishak Bharati Cooperative Limited (KRIBHCO) incorporated in 1985, are the two cooperative sector undertakings under the administrative control of the Department of Fertilizers.

IFFCO has four operating units, one each at Kalol and Kandla in Gujarat and Phulpur and Aonla in Uttar Pradesh. KRIBHCO has a gas-based urea-ammonia plant at Hazira in Gujarat with a capacity to produce 14.50 lakh tonnes of urea per annum. The combined installed capacity of IFFCO and KRIBHCO is 15.31 lakh tonnes of nitrogen and 3.09 lakh tonnes of phosphate.

The assumption on the savings front is that the public sector would be able to return positive savings to the tune of 2.8 per cent of GDP. Currently, the net dissavings in the government sector in in the order of one and-a-half per cent, while the public secor undertakings return positive savings, amounting to a little over three and-a-half per cent GDP.

However, the scope for the latter to increase further is limited, as the share of public sector units' (PSUs) output in the GDP gradually declines in the wake of reforms that seek to confer a larger role to private capital. In fact, it would not be surprising if the PSU savings as percentage of GDP actually came down. With public sector saving at 2.8 per cent of GDP, the government (both at the Centre and the States) needs to bring down their dissavings substantially. It implies a substantial curb on profligacy sundrome, further fiscal consolidation and an impressive step-up in tax revenues.

The Ninth Plan of Rs. 27.2 lakh crore at 1996-97 base prices would have about 40 per cent of the resources allocated for the public sector. This would include Rs. 3.76 lakh crore as budgetary support. But then, growth is not just a question of gross investment—its sectoral distribution as also the policies that direct it are equally relevant. And, it is here that the government holds the key entirely. In fact, any particular level of budgetary support to the Plan makes little sense without refernce to its sectoral allocation. Budget funds are required to meet the investment needs of sectors that will not attract private funds, particularly the social sectors. The government must, therefore, first prioritze the sectors and then discuss the amount it would invest during the Plan period.

While raising resources would be the major problem during the Ninth Plan period, the Centre and the States wouls have to increase tax rates, remove the loopholes in tax laws and improve collection. There is need for steps by the Centre and the States to increase tax-GDP ratio for additional resource mobilization. The suggestion made by the West Bengal Chief Minister, Mr. Jyoti Basu, for tapping black money sources to raise resources and to ensure that people having black money are forced to part with a slice of their ill-gotten wealth for developmental purposes is worth considering.

Among the various policies enunciated for restructuring of the PSUs, a major step involved the disinvestment of a part of Government equities in selected public undertakings for improving their performance as well as to increase their public accountability by broad basing their management and ownership. In the process of disinvestment, a major step taken by the government has been to set up the Disinvestment Commission for working out the terms and conditions as well as modalities pertaining to disinvestment of public equities. At present the government contemplates restructuring of equity in 40 major PSUs, including blue-chip companies like ONGC, GAIL, SAIL, MTNL, IPCL, NTPC, BEML, Power Grid, NHPC, IOC, IBP and Bongalgoan Refineries. While the Commission is to determine the modalities of disinvestment, the actual sale of PSU shares would be done through Deptt. of Public Enterprises (DPE). The Commission also intends to identify the non-core PSUs where the Government may even disinvest by more than 50 per cent and may have minority ownership.

Under auspices of the National Renewal Fund (NRF) set up in February 1992, for mobilising funds to assist voluntary retired persons from PSUs in undergoing re-training and re-deployment, Rs. 252 crore and Rs. 217 crore were released in 1994-95 and 1995-96, respectively. An estimated number of 87,800 workers have opted for voluntary retirement so far and a major portion of NRF has been utilised in the textile sector.

Indistrial relations have shown a steady improvement in the years follow the economic reforms. Mandays lost due to strikes and lockouts declined significantly from 22.97 million in 1992-93 to 17.99 million in 1995-96. This was mainly due to improvement in the industrial relations situation in cotton, engineering, coal and non-coal mining, beverages, tobacco & tobacco products, jute and rubber industries. During 1992-96, industrial unrest was witnessed mainly in the states of Andhra Pradesh, Gujarat, Tamil Nadu and Maharashtra, Government's proactive role through timely and effective conciliation of industrial disputes and involvement of the social partners in the formulation and implementation of labour and industrial relations policies and programmes has successfully harmonised the interests of employers and workers.

First company legislation in India was an Act for registration of joint stock companies enacted in 1850. This was followed by the Companies Act, 1913. As a result of recommendations of a committee under the chairmanship of C.H. Bhabha to make suggestions for company law reform, the Companies Act, 1956 was enacted as a Central lefislation. Prior to enactment of this Act, administration of companies' legislation was the responsibility of the state governments.

The Companies Act, 1956 has been in force for the last 38 years and during this period it has been amended over 16 times. Amendments of 1969, 1974, 1977 and 1988 are of special importance. By the amendment Act of 1969, system of appointing managing agencies or secretaries or treasurers in companies was abolished. Under the 1974 amendment, powers of High Court relating to certain sections of the Companies Act were transferred to Company Law Board. Scope of Section 43A was enlarged so as to treat large private limited companies as deemed public limited companies. A new Section 58A was inserted to regulate acceptance of deposits by companies. Section 108A to Section 108H were introduced to check take-over bids by large groups.

The 1977 amendment inserted, inter alia Section 634A enabling Company Law Board to enforce its orders under Section 17, 18, 19, 79 141 and 186 of the Act as a decree of a court of law. The Companies Act, 1956 provides various powers to Central Government and Company Law Board, to monitor, regulate and control the affairs of companies.

Salient features of the 1988 amendments are: (a) setting up of an independent Company Law Board to exercise such judicial and quasi-judicial functions as are presently being exercised either by Court or Central government and proposed to be transferred to that Board; (b) dispensing with Government approval for managerial appointments and remuneration, subject to fulfilment of certain statutory guidelines which are proposed to be incorporated in the Act itself; (c) delinking of rates of depreciation from rates specified under the Income Tax Act and laying down rates of depreciation in the Act itself to reflect true and fair view of the state of affairs of the company; (d) protecting the interest of investors by providing for intervention by Company Law Board against non-payment of public deposits and certain other matters, compulsory redemption of preference shares in certain cases, requiring companies to disclose reasons for refusal to register transfer of shares, protecting the rights of thee transfere pending mutation of his name in the register of members, and also compulsory lilsting of all public issues; (e) reducing unnecessary cost or burden by requiring companies to attach only an abridged version * for disclosure of information relating to conservation of energy, technology absorption, foreign exchange earnings and outgo as well as particulars of employees having some minimum stake in the company and drawing remuneration in excess of that drawn by managerial personnel.

The number of joint stock companies, both Government and non-Government incorporated under the Companies Act, 1956 and at work in India as on 31 March 1994 was 3,08,324. Of these 3,05,625 were limited by shares, 349 with unlimited liability and 2,350 were limited by guarantee or were associations not for profit. The 3,05,625 companies limited by shares have paid up capital of Rs. 1,04,890.8 crore. These comprised 38,000 public limited companies and 2,67,625 private limited companies with paid up capital of Rs. 70,112.1 and Rs. 34,778.7 crore respectively.

The primary objective of the Government's policy for Small and Tiny Enterprises would be to impart more vitality and growth impetus to the sector to enable it to contribute its mite fully to the economy particularly in terms of out put, employment and exports. In this context, it is heartening to note that at the end of the 7th Plan period the small scale sector accounted for mearly 35 per cent of the gross value of the out put in the manufacturing sector and over 40 per cent of the total exports from the country.

It also provided employment opportunties to around 12 million people. To ensure the growth of the Small and Tiny sector the Government proposes to review and modify all Statutes, regulations and procedures wherever necessary, to ensure that their operations do not militate against the interest of small and village enterprises.

As mentioned earlier in this paper, manufacturing units with an investment and plant and machinery up to * 75 lakhs and units which are willing to undertake an export obligation to the extent of 30 per cent of their annual production by 3rd year with an investment of Rs. up to 75 lakhs are eligigle for small scale registration. The investment limit in respect of Tiny Enterprises has been increased from Rs. 2 lakhs to Rs. 5 lakhs. With the objective of providing support to the service sector in view of its potential for generating employment, it has been decided that in future all industry related service and business enterprises irrespective of their location would be recognised as small scale industries and their investment ceiling would correspond to those of Tiny Enterprises.

Units in the small scale sector (other than Tiny Enterprises) would be entitled to benefits like preference in land allocation, power connection, access to facilities for skill/technology upradation. Tiny enterprises would in addition to these benefits will also be eligble for additional support including easier access to institutional finance, priority in the Government purchase programme and relaxation from certain provisions of labour laws.

Inadequate access to credit-both short—term and long—term remains a perennial problem facing the small scale sector. Emphasis would henceforth shift from subsidiese/cheap credit, except for specified target groups, and efforts would be made to ensure both adequate flow of credit on a normative basis, and the quality of its delivery, for viable operations of this sector. A special monitoring agency would be set up to oversee that the genuine credit needs of the small scale sector are fully met. To provide access to the capital market and to encourage modernisation and technlogical upgradation, it has been decided to allow equity participation by other industrial undertakings in the SSI, not exceeding 24 per cent of the total shareholding. this would also provide a powerful boost to ancillarisation and subcontracting, leading to expansion of employment opportunities.

Regulatory provisions relating to the management of private limited companies are being liberalised. A Limited Partnership Act will be introduced to enhance the supply of risk capital to the small scale sector. Such an Act would limit the financial liability of the new and non-active partners/entrepreneurs to the capital invested.

A beginning has been made towards solving the problems of delayed payments to small industries by setting up of factoring services through Small Industries Development Bank of India (SIDBI). Network of such services would be set up throughout the country and operated through commercial banks. A suitable legislation will be introduced to ensure prompt payment of small industries' bills.

To facilitate location of industries in rural/backward areas and to promote stringer linkages between agriculture and industry, a new Scheme of Integrated Infrastructural Develpoment (including Technological Back-up Services) for Small Scale Industries would be implemented with the active participation of State Government and Financial Institutions. A beginning in this direction will be made this year itself.

A Technology Development Cell (TDC) would be set up in the Small Industries Development Organisation

(SIDO) which would provide technology inputs to improve productivity and competitiveness of the products of the small scale sector. The TDC would coordinate the activities of the Tool Rooms, Process-cum-Product Development Centres (PPDCs), existing as well as to be established under SIDO, and would also interact with the other industrial research and development organisations to achieve its objectives.

Adequacy and equitable distribution of indigenous and imported raw material would be ensured to the small scale sector, particularly the tiny sub-sector. Policies would be so designed that they do not militate against entry of new units. Based on the capacity needs, Tiny/Small Scale Units would be given priority in allocation of indigenous raw materials.

A proper and adequate arrangement for delivery of total package of incentives and services at the District level will be evolved and implemented.

Inspite of the vast domestic market, marketing remains a problem area for Small and Tiny Enterprises. Mass consumption labour intensive products are predominantly being marketed by the organised sector. The Tiny/Small Scale Sector will be enabled to access existing support mechanism. Market promotion would be undertaken through cooperative/public sector institutions, other specialised/professional marketing agencies and consortia approach, backed up by such incentives as considered necessary.

National Small Industries Corporation (NSIC) would concentrate on marketing of mass consumption items under common brand name and organic links between NSCI and State Small Industries Development Corporations (SSIDCs) would be established.

Government recognises the need to widen and

deepen complementarity in production programmes of large/medium and small industrial sectors. Parts, components, sub assemblies, etc. required by large public/private sector undertakings would be encouraged for production in a techno-economically viable manner through small scale ancillary units. Industry associations would be encouraged to establish subcontracting exchanges, in addition to strengthening the existing ones under the SIDO. Emphasis would also be laid on promotion of a viable and competitive component market.

Though the small scale sector is making significant contribution to total exports both direct and indirect, a large potential remains untapped. SIDO has been recognised as the nodal agency to support the small scale industries in export promotion. An Export Development Centre would be set up in SIDO to serve the small scale industries through its network of field offices to further augment export activities of this sector.

A greater degree of awareness to produce goods and services conforming to national and international standards would be created among the small scale sector.

Industry Associations would be encouraged and supported to establish quality counselling and common testing facilities. Technology Informaton Centres to provide updated knowledge on technology and markets would be established.

Where non-conformity with quality and standards involves risk to human life and public health, compulsory quality control would be enforced.

Are-oriented programme of modernisation and technological upgradation aimed at improving productivity, efficiency and cost effectiveness in the small scale sector would be pursued. Specific industries in large concentrations/clusters would be identified for studies in conjunction with SIDBI and other banks. Such studies will establish commercial viability of modernisation prescriptions, and financial support would be provided for modernisation of these industries on a priority basis.

Indian Institutes of Technology (IITs) and selected Regional/other Engineering Colleges will serve as Technological Information, design and Development Centres in their respective command areas.

Government will continue to support first generation entrepreneurs thrugh training and other measures. Large number of EDP trainers and motivators will be trained to significantly expand the Entrepreneurship Development Programmes (EDP). Industry Associations would also be encouraged to participate in this venture effectively.

EDP would be built into the curricula of vocational and other degree level courses. Women entrepreneurs will receive support through special training programmes. Definition of "Women Enterprises" would be simplified. The present stipulation regarding employment of majority of women workers would be dispensed with and units in which women entrepreneurs have majority shareholding and management control, would be defined as "Women Enterprises".

Additional employment opportunities would be generated through training of multi-disciplinary barefoot managers to suit special requirements of the small scale sector.

The persistent complaint of small scale units of being subjected to a large number of Acts and Laws, being required to maintain a number of registers and submit returns, and face an army of inspectors, would be attended to within a specified time frame of three months.

Procedures would be simplified, bureaucratic controls effectively reduced, unnecessary interference eliminated an paper work cut down to the minimumto enable the entrepreneur to concentrate on production and marketing function.

The Government has also announced a number of steps for promoting Handloom sector, handicrafts sector and other village industries.

A number of organisations are engaged in exploration and development of mineral resources in India. These include Geolgical survey of India (GSI), Indian Bureau of Mines (IBM) and a number of public sector undertakings under the administrative control of the Ministry of Mines.

Geological Survey of India functions as the premier national organisation for earth science, entrusted with the task of scientific survey and research for locating mineral resources (except oil, natural gas and atomic minerals), systematic generation and continous updating of geoscience information through ground, airborne and marine survey, the entire gamut of activities being related to multifarious developmental needs of the country. The survey operates within the ambit of its charter 1873 and priorities laid down by the Government.

The other important functions of the organisation cover management of natural hazards like earthquake, floods, landslides, volcanism etc., providing geotechnical advice to all the major civil engineering, communication and urban development projects, geoenvironmental resource appraisal, upgradation of geoscientific expertise through training. The results of GSI investigations are documented in the form of scientific and technical reports, professional papers, maps, inventories and various types of publications.

The survey with its central headquarters at Calcutta, functions through six geographically based regions, three activity based Wings (Marine, Coal and Airborne Survey) and one training Institute. In each of the region/wings towards * greater collaboration and setting up of consultancy and commercial endeavours in the third world countries.

The Indian Bureau of Mines (IBM) is the national organisation under Ministry of Mines and engaged in promotion, conservation and scientific development of mineral resources of the country other than coal, petroleum and natural gas, atomic minerals and minor minerals. It performs regulatory functions, namely enforcement of Mines and Minerals (Regulation & Development Rules and the provision of Environmental Protection Act.

It also undertakes scientific techno-economic, research-orientid studies in various aspects such as geological, mining ore beneficiation and environment. IBM provides technical consultancy services to the mining industry for geological appraisal of mineral resources and preparation of feasibility reports of mining projects including beneficiation plants. It prepares mineral maps and countrywide inventory of minerals resources of leasehold and freehold areas.

IBM also functions as data bank for mines and minerals and publishes statistical periodicals and brings out technical publications/monogrphs on individual mineral commodities and bulletins on different connected subjects. it advises the Central and state governments on all aspects of mineral industry, trade and legislation. It imparts training to technical and non-technical officials of IBM and also persons from mineral industry and other agencies in India and abroad. IBM is organised into six functional agencies in India and abroad. IBM is organised into six functional divisions. It has its headquarters at Nagpur and 11 regional offices and well equipped ore-dressing laboratories and Pilot Plant at Nagpur, besides, two regional ore-dressing laboratories at Ajmer and Bangalore. IBM also has a big Central Library with about 61,000 books.

Public sector

Minral Exploration Corporation Limited (MECL) was created in 1972 with the main objective of bridging the gap between the disc overy of mineral prcspect and its eventual exploitation. Its identified major functions are to plan, promote, organise and implement programme for the exploration of mineral resources and to perform such functions as Central Government may from time to time, assign to the company in connection with exploration of the mineral resources in and outside the country.

The Corporation has its headquarters at Nagpur. MECL has fulfilled its main objective by establishing over 55,000 million tonnes of reserves of higher confidence for veriety of minerals. The drilling capacity of 72,000 m per annum at the time of inception in 1972 has increased to 4.25 lakh metre of drilling and mining capacity has increased from 1200 mtr in 1972 to 9000 m in the last year of Seventh Five Year Plan. During 1993-94, the turnover of the company was Rs. 40.73 crore.

Bharat Aluminium Company Limited (BALCO) was incorporated on 27 November 1965 as the first primary aluminium producing undertaking in the public sector. The Company is operating Korba Aluminium Complex in Bilaspur district of Madhya Pradesh and Bidhanbag Unit in Asanosl in west Bengal. It has a capacity to produce one lakh tonnes of aluminium metal/products. During the past few years, the Company's production of saleable metal/products has been about 92,000 tonnes per annum.

Its net profit has been going up steadily and during 1994-95, it earned a net profit of Rs. 90.51 crore (provisional). The new projects of the Company include installation of a new Cold Rolling Mill having an installed capacity to produce 40,000 TPA of thin quality sheets/coils. The Comapny is also in the process of modernisation of their smelter plant at Korba for increased productivity and reduction of power consumption which is a major factor in input costs.

National Aluminium Company Limited (NALCO) was incorporated on 7 January 1981 with the objective to produce alumina and aluminium. Its registerd office is at Bhubaneswar. It operates a bauxite mine to raise 24 lakh tonnes per annum of bauxite from the Parnchpatnali (Koraput) deposits, an eight lakh tonnes per annum alumina refinery at Damanjodi (Koraput), a 2,18,000 tonnes per annum aluminium smelter at Angul (Dhenkanal) and six 120 MW captive power plants at Angul to feed the smelter. Aluminium Pechiney of France was the technical consultants for the project and had supplied the technical know-how and basic engineering package.

NALCO received ISO 9002 Certification from IROS for Alumina Refinery on 21 November 1994 and ISO 9002 Certification for quality system for Smelter Plan in March 1995 from RWTUV. Highest production of calcined alumina of 81,000 MT during January 1995 exceeding the rated capacity. NALCO produced 1,78,072 tonnes of aluminium and earned net profit of Rs. 294.62 (provisional) during the same period.

Hindustan inc Limited (HZL) was incorporated on 10 January 1966 to take over operations of the earstwhile Metal Corporation of India Limited and to develop mining and smelting capacities to substantially meet the domestic demand of zinc and lead metals. With headquarters at Udaipur, HZL's operations are spread over in the states of Rajasthan, Andhra Pradesh, Orissa and Bihar consisting of five mines with a total lead-zinc ore production capacity of 3.04 million tpa and four smelters with combined installed capacity of 1,49,000 tpa zinc and 65,000 tpa lead besides a rock phosphate and tungsten mine. The company offers a wide range of zinc and lead metal grades to its customers, besides a range of by-products.

The production of zinc metal by the company during the last four years has ranged between 84,600 tpa and 1,19,810 tpa. The lead production during the same period has ranged between 30,300 tpa and 34,500 tpa. The sales turnover of the company during 1994-95 was Rs. 97,274 lakh and its net profit (after tax) during the same period was Rs. 7,643 lakh.

HZL signed a Memorandum of Understanding with M/s. Niugini Mining Limited.Australia, to identify gold resources in India and later on if resources are found viable, to set up a joint venture. It has also signed an MoU with M/s. BHP Minerals, Austrails, for exploration and development of base and procious metals in Rajasthan. Besides, HZL and BRGM, France, have reached an agreement with Vietnam Rare and Precious Metal Corporation (VMC) for setting up of joint venture for exploration and development of Pac Lang Gold Prospect in Vietnam.

Hindustan Copper Limited (HCL) is the sole producer of primary copper metal in the country. It was incorporated on 7 November 1967, to take over from the National Mineral Development Corporation, projects, schemes and studies pertaining to exploration, exploitation, mining and smelting of copper. In 1972, the erstwhile Indian Copper Corporation Limit, a company incorporated in England was nationalised and merged with HCl. The main projects of the company are: (i) Khetri Copper Complex (KCC) in Rajasthan comprising Khetri, Kolihan, Chandmari and Dariba mines (since closed), concentrators at Dariba (since closed) and Khetri, Metallurgical and fertilizer plants at Khetri; (ii) Indian Copper Complex (ICC) at Ghatsila in Bihar comprising Mosaboni, Fathargora, Kendadih and Rakha Mines, three concentrators at Mosaboni, Moubhandar (since closed) and Rakha and metallurgical plants for copper and by-product recovery at Moubhandari (iii) Malanjkhand Copper Project (MCP) at Malanjkhand in Madhya Pradesh comprising an open pit mine, concentrator and leach copper plant; and (iv) Taloja Copper Project (TCP) at Taloja in Maharashtra for conversion of cathodes both imported and part of our own into continuous cast copper wirerods as value added product.

The company produces primary copper products in the form of cathodes, wirebars, wirerods and is also engaged in manufacturing of single super phosphate, sulphuric acid, gold, silver, selenium, tellurium, palladium, copper sulphate and nickel sulphate as by-products.

The current operation plants of the company are to produce and market about 70.000 Mt copper in different forms out of which 45,000 MT of refined copper is produced from indigenous ore resources. With the changed economic scenario in the country, HCL has initiated process of restructuring of companies to remain competitive. During 1994-95, the turnover of the company was Rs. 932.95 and its production of refined copper was 46,134 MT.

Bharat Gold Mines Limited operates the world famous century old Kolar Gold Mines in Karnataka State. The company was nationalised in 1956 and was incorporated as a public sector company under the

Department of Mines, Government of India in March 1972. Though the gold mining is the principal activity of the company, as a corporate stategy, it has diversified into the field of mine construction and contract works, manufacture of mining machinery and components of equipment.

The company has three major activities namely: (i) Gold mining: Two mines in Kolar Gold Fields, Karntaka-Mysore Champion Amalgamated mine and Nundydroog mine, and three mines in Andhra Pradesh, Yeppamana mine, (Anantapur); Chigargunta mine; and Old Bisanatham mine, (Chittoor); (ii) Mine Project and Construction Division-Taking up mine construction and development works for other mining (coal and metal mines) industries all over India, and (iii) Workshop Diversification-The workshops manufacture mining machineries and components of certain equipment and undertake jobbing works, like machining and fabrication for major industries in the country.

The company's registered office is at Koar Gold Fields and its liaison office is at New Delhi. In 1994-95, the company produced 650.28 kg of gold.

The continued financial losses over the decade has resulted in the company being declared as a sick industry and consequently referred to Board for Industrial and Financial Reconstruction (BIFR) who have appointed ICICI as Operating Agency to formulate a rehabilitation package envisaging increase in gold production from the existing shallow mines to ensure economic viability, exploration and exploitation of gold from the BGML lease-hold areas in collaboration with a suitable joint venture partner and to recover gold from old mill tailings accumulated over the years by constructing a suitable gold recovery plant by BGML.

Sikkim Mining Corporation was established as joint venture of Sikkim State and Government of India in 1960 by proclamation of erstwhile "Sikkim Darbar". the objective of the Corporation is to mine multimental ore for production of copper, lead and zinc concentrates. The Corporation has only one mine (Bhotang Mine) Situated at Rangpo (East Sikkim). During 1994-95, the Corporation produced 270 mt tonnes of copper concentrate, 85 mt of lead concentrate and 568 mt of zinc concentrate. Zinc concentrate is being sold to M/s. Hindustan Zinc Ltd. since April 1994. Hindustan Copper Limited has stopped taking copper concentrate, M/s HAMCO Mining and Smelting Limited, Calcutta, has lifted 3,500 tonnes of lead, 200 tonnes of copper and 200 tonnes of zono concentrates on trial basis in the year 1994-95.

The National Mineral Policy, 1993, announced on 5 March 1993, in brief, had dispensed with the reservation of all the minerals reserved for exclusive exploitation by public sector and also for the first time, sought to invite foreign investment in the mining sector. The amendments to the Mines and Minerals (Regulation & Development) Act, 1957 seek to further elaborate the principles enunciated in the National Mineral Policy by, among others, devolving more powers to the state governments, providing greater stability of tenure in mining leases and by accelerating inflow of private capital, both domestic and foreign, as also the state-of-the-art technology into the mineral sector.

The amended Act has deleted 15 minerals hitherto listed in the First Schedule of the MM (R&D) Act, 1957 requiring prior approval of the Central Government before the state government could grant a prospecting licence of a mining lease. The minerals so deleted are apatite and phosphatic ores, barytes, dolomite, gypsum, kyanite, magnesite, molybdenum, nickel, platimum and other precious metals, sillimanite, silver, sulphur and its ores, tin, tungsten and vanadium ore. With this deletion (excepting the atomic minerals and fuel minerals), there would only be 11 minerals left for which the state government would require prior approval of the Central Government. These are asbestos, bauxite, chrome ore, copper ore, gold, iron ore, lead, limestone (except where it is used in kilns for the manufacute of lime as building materials) manganese ore, precious stones and zinc. the amended Act has removed any restriction on equity holding by foreign nationals in a mining company.

As of now, any company registered or incorporated in India can apply for a prospecting licence of a mining lease from the concerned state government. For the first time, a minimum period of lease of 20 years, has been made mandatory. The maximum period for grant of lease has been increased to 30 years.

Further renewals are possible with approval of the Central Government. The period for which prospecting licence can be granted has been increased to three years and these licences can be renewed at the discretion of the state governments so that the total period does not exceed five years. The amended Act also provides that no appeal or revision will lie to the Central Government against orders passed by the state governments with regard to minor minerals. State governments have also been empowered to terminate leases of minor minerals without prior approval of the Central Government. The amended Act also introduces a new section, whch gives powers to carry out searches to check unauthorised mining.

The Act, was amended to increase the period before which a lease can lapse from one year to two years. In addition, the amendment also provides that notifications issued by state governments under their minor minerals concession rules must be placed before the State Legislature and also empowers the Central Government to modify leases not in conformity with the Act to bring them in line with the provisions of the MMR&D Act, 1957.

The history of modern iron and steel industry in India began in 1870 when the Bengal Iron Works Company set up its plants at Kulti in West Bengal. However, the first effort at large scale production got underway when the Tata Iron Steel Company (TISCO) was set up at Jamshedpur in 1907. This was followed by the establishment of Indian Iron and Steel Company (IISCO) at Burnpur in 1919.

The first unit in public sector now known as Visvesvaraya Iron and Steel Limited (VISL) started functioning at Bhadravati in 1923. After Independence, though development of steel industry was considered during the First Plan, it was only during the Second Plan period that efforts were made to set up three integrated steel plants each with 10 lakh ingot tonnes capacity at Bhilai, Durgapur and Rourkela. An expansion programme to double the capacity of the two private sector steel plants, namely, TISCO and IISCO to 20 lakh tonnes ad 10 lakh tonnes respectively was also taken up.

The three plants in the public sector came into existance in stages between 1956 and 1959 and the expansion of the private sector plants was completed in 1959. During the Third Five Year Plan, emphasis was laid on the expansion of the three public sector plants and preparation of plans to set up three more steel plants at Salem (Tamil Nadu). Vijaynagar (Karnataka) and Visakhapatnam (Andhra Pradesh) to create additional steel production capacity in the Fifth Plan.

Steel Authority of India Limited (SAIL) is a wholly-owned government undertaking. It is responsible for the management of steel plants at Bhilai, Durgapur and Rourkela, Bokaro and Burnpur and also the Alloy Steel Plant at Durgapur an the Salem Steel Plant. The management of IISCO was taken over the Government on 14 July 1976 with a view to improving its working. The company is now a wholly-owned subsidiary of SAIL. SAIL took over Maharashtra Elektrosmelt Limited, a mini steel plant producing ferro-manaanese and steel in January 1986. Visvesvaraya Iron and Steel Limited, a unit controlled by the Karnataka Government was taken over by SAIL in August 1989.

Authorised capital of SAIL and paid up capital, as on 31 March 1995 are Rs. 5,000 crore and Rs. 3,985.89 crore respectively. The turnover during 1994-95 was Rs. 13,688.54 crore (excluding IISCO). Production of crude steel, saleable steel and pig iron from steel plants under SAIL (excluding IISCO) during 1993-94 and 1994-95.

Apart from the integrated steel plants, steel is also produced by electric arc furnace units which are popularly known as mini steel plants, from steel scrap/ sponge iron. While integrated steel plants mainly produce mild steel in bulk quantities, the mini steel plants produce mild seel as well as alloy steels including stainless steels. From this sector, crude steel production during 1994-95 was 2.9 million tonnes (provisional).

The New Industrial Policy announced in July 1991 has removed iron and steel from the list of industries reserved for the public sector, and also exmpted it from the requirements of compulsory licensing. Enterpreneurs are, therefore, free to set up steel plants of any capacity, subject to certain locational restrictions.

Iron and steel has also been placed in the list of high priority industries where, subject to certain conditions, automatic approvals are available for foreign equity upto 51 per cent, and for technology agreements upto specified limits. There has been a very positive response from the entrepreneurs. A capacity of about 7.5 million tonnes for producing various categories of steel involving an investment of about Rs. 13,142 crore is in various stages of implementation.

Rashtriya Ispat Nigam Limited was incorporated as a public sector company in February 1982 to implement construction of the first shorebased Integrated Steel Plant in th country located at Visakhapatnam, Andhra Pradesh. The project has been completed in two stages: first stage was completed by March 1992 and the second and final stage by July 1992.

Visakhapatnam Steel Plant (VSP) is the most sophisticated modern integrated steel plant in the country. Some of the most modern technologies adopted in the plant are: seven metre tall coke ovens, dry quenching of coke with auxiliary power generation facilities, 3200 CuM blas furnaces, conveyor charging and bell-less top charging for blast furnaces, cent per cent continuous casting of liquid steel and sophisticated high speed rolling mills. VSP's manpower, considering its size is lowest in the Indian steel industry. Though the production in Visakhapatnam Steel Plant commenced in the year 1991-92, 1993-94 was the first full year of integrated operation.

Visakhapatnam Steel Plant has achieved high levels of techno-economic and operating performances during 1994-95 creating records in the Indian steel industry and surpassing the DPR Norms. On the marketing front, VSP ended the year with a turnover of about Rs. 2,266 crore, which is 19 per cent higher than that of the previous year. Domestic sales of steel showed substantial increase with sales volume registering 1.2 million tonnes, a 43 per cent growth over 1993-94. Exports accounted for 4.65 lakh tonnes of iron and steel with a total realisation of Rs. 471

crore in foreign exchange. By-product sales registered a turnover of Rs. 147 crore which is 65 per cent higher than what was achieved in the previous year. VSP made a cash profit of Rs. 55 crore (provisional), for the first time, as against a cash los of Rs. 233 crore made in 1993-94.

At present, rubber goods industry comprises of 32 tyre units, 220 medium scale units, 5,500 small scale units and an equal number of units in the tiny sector. It offers direct and indirect employment to over seven lakh people. There is an investment of about Rs. 3,500 crore and a turnover of over Rs. 7,000 crore in this industry. The major rubber goods produced by the industry are tyres and tubes of all kinds, surgical gloves, prophylactics, conveyor and vee belts, instruments, hose pipes, sport goods etc. Tyres and tubes constitute the most important segment of this industry. Of the total investment, over Rs. 2,000 crore have been in the tyre and tubes industry. This industry has been identified as of extreme focus for export purposes.

The export of tyres and tubes which was Rs. 593 crore in 1993-94 is expected to reach Rs. 750 crore in 1994-95 and Rs. 1,000 crore by 1995-96. The exports of rubber goods other than tyres and tubes are also steadily growing.

Over the years, engineering industries in the country have registered a phenomenal growth to generate a strong base in a wide-range of heavy and light engineering industries covering a broad spectrum of capital goods and consumer durable products. Bulk of capital goods required for power projects, fertilizer plants, cement plants, steel plants, mining equipment and petro-chemical plants are being met from indigenous production. Construction machinery and equipment for irrigation project, diesel engines, pumps and tractors for agriculture, vehicles, etc., transport are also being met from within the country. Engineering industries have also demonstrated their capacity to manufacture large size plants and equipment for virous sectors such as power generation, fertilizers and cement.

Machine Tool industry is the backbone of entire engineering sector. This industry which till few years back was confined to the manufacture of conventional machine holding has now geared itself to meet the growing challenge of a diverse requirement from the user sector.

Heavy electrical industry comprises equipment used for the generation, transmission, distribution and utilisation of power. It includes items such as generators, boilers, tubines, transformers, switchgears etc. The indigenous industry is equipped to meet the entire domestic requirement. The established capacity in the country for manufacture of thermal and hydro-power generating equipment is around 4,500 mw and 1,345 mw respectively. Most of these capacities are in the public sector, in companies such as BHEL. The entire industry has been delicensed under the New Indusrial Policy announced by the Government of India. Also under the new Policy, these items qualify for automatic approval as regard to foreign collaborations.

Stream and hydro turbines are manufactured both in the public and private sector The total capacity is over 7,000 mw. The public sector undertaking BHEL has the largest capacity. Steam turbines upto 500 mw unit rating are being manufactured by BHEL. It also manufactures gas turbines.

Boliers of both the categories, namely, for industrial and power applications are being produced in the country. For power boilers, BHEL is capable of making boilers for super thermal power plants. M/s. ABL Durgapur, is a major unit manufacturing power boilers.

There are 19 manufactures of industrial boilers in the country. The production of fludised bed boilers using biomass, agricultural waste, inferior grades of coal etc., has also started both for process application as well as for generating power.

There are 33 units in the organised sector manufacturing power and distribution transformers. The technology and design of power transformers manufactured in the country are comparable with the international standards. Manufacturing facilities for dry type distribution transformers have been established in th country. The technology and manufacturing facilities for amorphous core transformers and aluminium foil wound transformers are being established.

In the context of power system development in evolving a National Grid by end of current Plan period, conceted efforts are on for strengthening the transmission system by execution of 400 KV lines, introducing HVDC back-to-back tie lines, phased conversion of AC lines into DC lines and implementing load despatch and communication links besides system improvement measures by installing adequate reactive compensation system and PF correction capacitor banks.

AC transmission in 800 KV class has been adopted as the standard for the next higher level. Indigenous industry is technology sufficient in transmission system upto 400 KV reactive compensation system upto 220 KV and is in the process of indigenisation of HVDC technology and development of 800 KV class equipments. A total switchover to all Alluminium Alloy Conductors (AAAC), realising its techno-economic benefits, would give a boost to this sector.

The electrical industry covers a wide range of products which includes white goods (refrigerators, washing machines, air-conditiones, etc.), house-hold, electrical appliances, electrical, fans, storage batteries, dry cells, power cables, telecommunication cables, electrical motors and electric lamps. The installed capacity is considered adequate to meet the domestic demand as well as exports. Under the new industrial policy, the entire industry has been delicensed. Many of the electrical items like electric motors, jelly filled cables, optic fibre cables and pumping sets also qualify for 51 per cent foreign equity and automatic foreign collaboration under the new industrial policy.

In the field of telecommunication, capacity has also been created for manufacture of optical fibre cables. Hindustan Cables Limited, a Government of India undertaking, and the Madhya Pradesh State Electronic Development Corporation, an undertaking of the Government of Madhya Pradesh, have been permitted to establish capacities for the manufacture of OFC to the extent of 40,000 and 20,000 fibre km per annum respectively.

Keeping in view the safety and quality aspects of household electric appliances, Government have introduced compulsory ISI marking in respect of electrical immersion heaters, electrical iron, electrical stove and plugs and sockets.

Various steps have been initiated to ensure adequate testing facilities and availability of quality raw materials and components to the manufactures in order to help them conform to the requirements of the said scheme. There has been a greater consumer awareness about the quality and safetyof these goods.

The need for energy conservation has ensured greater focus in the manufacture of energy efficient electrical lamps. The industry is receiving adequate encouragement from the Government. A number of foreign collaborations have already been apporoved for manufacture of energy efficial lamps.

In the storage battery industry, some new units are coming up. The process of upgradation of technology in this industry is continuously benefiting the customers. The industry has started providing batteries to Maruti Premier 113 NE and Contessa Classic apart from light commercial vehicles.

The crane industry has a good potential for growth in the coming year in view of increased port and container handling activities and other projects like steel plant modernisation. Considerable investment is this area has been made by the indigenous crane manufactures. By and large the indigenous manufactures are capable of meeting the demand. The industry is delicensed.

At present there are eight units in the country engaged in the manufacture of lifts and escalators. The present installed capacity of these units is of the order of 3000 Nos per annum. A new range of lifts known as Sky Climbers has been/is under manufacture indigenously. These lifts are used for maintenance of TPS boilers/ bridges etc., and are being produced for the first time.

As elsewhere in the world, there is an increasing shift in India to have large power houses particularly Super Thermal Power Stations. Consequently, while there would be fewer but larger power generating stations, the demand for transmission line towers for transmission of energy would grow substantially. There are at present 25 manufacturing units reporting production to Ministry of Industry. There is sufficient capacity available in the country for manufacture of different types of transmission line towers. The industry is delicensed subject to locational angle.

Paper is a vital and core industry for any country

and per capita paper consumption can be taken as a measure of growth and progress in areas related to industrial, cultural and educational activities. Per capita consumption in India is less than three kg as against more than 300 kg in highly developed countries.

The origin of the paper industry could be traced back to 1812 when first paper mill was set up at Serampur, West Bengal. At present there are more than 350 mills in the country with an annual installed capacity of around 37 lakh tonnes. A significant aspect of the paper industry is strong presence of smaller paper mills with an installed capacity of 33,000 tonnes per annum or less. They account for nearly 50 per cent of the total installed capacity and contribute about 50 per cent to the production of paper and paper board in the country.

Capacity utilisation of the paper industry has declined from 96.35 per cent in 1952 to about 60 per cent in 1994. Various reliefs and concessions have been extended in recent years to help the industry to improve its capacity utilisation and financial viability. These include liberalisation facility for import of raw materials, low excise on use of minimum 75 per cent non-conventional raw materials *viz.* bagasse, jute, wheat/rice straw, waste paper, etc., delicensing the manufacture of certain varieties of paper etc.

At present, the country is self-sufficient in respect of common varieties of writing and printing paper and paper board and only certain special varieties of papers are being imported. The import of paper has been brought under OGL and customs duty on import of paper has been reduced from 65 to 20 per cent in this year. The demand of paper and paper board up to the end of the Eighth Plan is likely to be met by some new mills, revival of the some of the closed mills, modernisation and expansion of some of the existing units. In order to encourage use ofnon-conventional raw material, paper units based on use of minimum 75 per cent pulp derived from bagasse, agricultural residues and other non-conventional raw materials have been exempted from industrial licensing subject to locational policy.

Until 1981, National Newsprint and Paper Mills recently known as *nepa* Limited which commenced in 1955 was the only unit in the country manufacturing newsprint. As on 1 January 1995, there are 22 newsprint mills in the country with an annual installed capacity of 5.50 lakh tonnes. However, one newsprint mills *viz.* rayalseema Paper Mills Ltd having an annual installed capacity of 20,000 TPA is lying closed.

Demand for newsprint is met by indigenous production supplemented by imports. Import of newsprint which was decanalised earlier, has been decontrolled with effect from 1 May 1995. Now, import of newsprint is under OGL. The customs duty on the import of newsprint has been abolished with effect from 25 July 1991 in respect of standard newsprint and with effect from 1 march 1992 in respect of glazed newsprint. The production of newsprint for 1994-95 was about 4.02 lakh tonnes.

Cement, an important infrastructure core industry, is one of the most advanced industries in the country. Till about a decade ago, the country was deficient in cement and it had to resort to import in order to fill the gap in supply. After the complete de-control of price and distribution on 1 March 1989 and introduction of other policy reforms, the cement industry has made rapid strides both in capacity/production and in production and process technology. At present there are 107 large plants with an installed capacity of about 79 million tonnes. In addition, there are about 250-300 mini cement plants with an estimated capacity of seven million tonnes. The total operative installed capacity is estimated to be around 86 million tonnes. In 1993-94, production of cement was 57.96 million tonnes against a target of 60 million tonnes. The Production target fixed for 1994-95 was 62 million tonnes. With a production of 62.35 million tonnes, the industry was able to achieve the target. The growth rate recorded during the year was 7.6 per cent. During the year the capacity utilitisation has also increased from 80 per cent in 1993-94 to 86 per cent.

India is producing different varieties of cement the ordinary portland cement (OPC), portland pozzolana cement (PPC), portland blaster furnace slag cement (PBFS), oil well cement, white cement, etc. These different varieties of cement are produced strictly under BIS specifications and the quality is comparable to the best of the world.

Apart from meeting the entire domestic demand for cement, the industry is also exporting a large quantity. The export of clinker and cement has increased from 0.36 million tonnes in 1990-91 to 1.18 million tonnes in 1992-93 and 2.85 million tonnes in 1993-94. The export in 1994-95 was to the tune of 3.38 million tonnes.

Utilising a part of the funds provided by the World Bank to the cement industry and the grant from DANIDA, Denmark, a Human Resource Development Project is being implemented for providing demand driven training to the operators, line managers and supervisors to enhance their skills for handling latest equipments.

Four regional training centres have been set up and equipped with various classroom equipments, special equipments, computers, books, manuals and other training aids at ACC, Jamul (M.P.), Dalmia Cement,

Dalmiapuram (T.N.), J.K. Cement, Nimbahera (Rajasthan) anmd Gujarat Ambuja, Ambuja Nagar (Gujarat). A large number of personnel of the cement industry and part-time trainers have already been trained in these RTCS. Fourteen training packages have already been developed abroad and 18 more are presently being developed.

Another innovative pilot project for bulk transportation and distribution of cement is being implemented with World Bank assistance at Kalamboli, New Bombay. Department of Industrial Policy and Promotion and the Associated Cement Companies Ltd. (ACC) are participating directly in the project. Under this project, special high.

The drugs and pharmaceuticals industry in India, during the last 40 years has shown tremendous progress if one takes into consideration the growth rate as seen in other developing countries. Today, India is in a position to meet 70 per cent of its requirement of bulk drugs and almost all its requirement of formulations. The industry continued to maintain the steady growth in terms of production as well as range of products in 1993-94 alslo. During 1994-95, the production of bulk drugs and formulations is estimated to be of the order of Rs. 1,518 crore and Rs. 7,935 crore respectively, showing a growth rate of 15 per cent over the previous year's production. In the case of individual drugs, where decrease in production has taken place, it is noted that factors like decline in demand and obsolescence have a significant impact.

The pharmaceutical industry in india has the capability of producing a wide range of bulk drugs, covering a large spectrum of technologies and almost all formulations. In fact, the country is almost fully self-reliant in terms of formulation technology. In the case of bulk drugs, the technologies include those for sulpha drugs, vitamins, hormones and a number of new synthetic drugs like Flumequine, Pefloxacin, Ramipiril Ketorolac, Lisinopirl etc.

Among the bulk drugs which are critical to the country's health needs, the two most important ones are Penicillin and Rifampicin. The basic stage production of Penicillin and Rifampicin has been steadily growing and almost half of the country's demand for these two important drugs is met by indigenous production.

Two public sector undertakings, namely, Hindustan Antibiotics Limited (HAL) and Indian Drugs and Pharmaceuticals Limited (IDPL), account for almost 90 per cent of the Penicillin production in the Country. In addition to one private sector unit, which had commenced production of Penicillin in the last years, three more Penicillin manufacturing units in the private sector, with an investment of about Rs. 500 crore, are expected to commence commercial production in 1995. The indigenous production of Penicillin is thus expected to almost double from the existing level to meet the country's demand in the coming years.

In addition to the two manufactures of inermediates of Rifampicin from the basic stage, which today meets about 50 per cent of the indigenous demand of this important anti-TB and anti-leprosy drug, industrial license has been issued to another unit to produce this drug from the basic stage.

In view of the experience gained over the years, the Government had felt the need to modify the existing Drug Policy, 1986 so as to bring it in consonance with the Industrial Policy, 1991 and the present EXIM Policy as also to simplify and streamline the existing pricing system. The salient features of the Modifications in Drug Policy, 1986 announced on the 15 September 1994 are: (i)

Abolition of Industrial Licencing for all bulk drugs, their intermediates and formulations thereof except in case of five bulk drugs reserved for manufacture in the public sector and bulk drugs produced by the use of recombinant DNA technology as well as those requiring in-vivo use of nucleic acid as the active principles; (ii) Foreign investment upto 51 per cent will be automatically permitted in the case of all bulk drugs, their intermediates and formulations; (iii) automatic approval, as per the industrial policy, for foreign technology agreements shall be given in the case of all bulk drugs, their intermediates and formulations, except those produced by the use of recombinant DNA techology; (iv) Measures to give further impetus to R&D in the During Sector are as follows: (a) A new drug which has not been produced elsewhere, if developed through indigenous R&D would be put outside price control for a period of 10 years from the date of commercial production in favour of the Company who undertook the R&D; (b) The Department of Chemicals and Petrochemicals would set up an Inter-Ministerial group to decide, within a set time frame, on measures to give further impetus to R&D in the Drug Sector, and (c) The Ministry of Health and Family Welfare would further steamline the required procedures and steps for the quick-evaluation and clearance of new durg applications, specially those developed through indigenous R&D; (v) The system of price control would be operated through a single list of price controlled drugs, selected on the basis of transparent and objective criteria as laid down in the Modifications in Drug Policy, 1986" and formulations based thereon with a MAPE of 100 per cent; (vi) In case of basic manufacture, higher by four per cent over the existing rates which are 14 per cent on net worth or 22 per cent on capital employed; (vii) To achieve uniformity in prices of widely used formulations, it has been decided that there should be ceiling on prices for commonlymarketed standard pack sizes of price controlled formulations and that it would be obligatory for all, including small scale units, to follow the prices so fixed; (viii) An independent body of experts, to be called the National Pharmaceutical Pricing Authority, will be entrusted with the task of price-fixation/revision and other related medicines which are taken out of price control. In case, the prices of these medicines rise unreasonably, the Government would take appropriate measures, incluing reclamping of price control. (x) A National Drug Authority would be set up by an Act of the Parliament, to be steered by the Ministry of Health and Family Welfare, to look after the quality control aspects, rational use of drugs and related matters; and (xi) To provide better focus to all matters relating to development and promotion of indigenous and other system of medicines, a separate Department would be created by the Ministry of Health and Family Welfare.

The Drugs (Prices Control) Order (DPCO), 1995 has been notified by the Government on 6 January 1995. This Order has now come into force in place of the DPCO, 1987. The new DPCo has taken into account the modifications in the Drug Policy, 1986 announced by the Government in September 1994 in regared to the price control on drugs and has been issued in exercise of the powers conferred on the Central Government in September 1994 in regard to the price control on drugs and has been issued in exercise of the powers conferred on the Central Government by Section 3 of the Essential Commodities Act, 1955.

Seventy six drugs have been identified for being kept in the First Schedule of the DPCO which lists the drugs to be kept under price control. Unlike the DPCO, 1987 now there is a single list of drugs under price control with a Maximum Allowable Post Manufacturing Expenses (MAPE) of 100 per cent. Twenty two drugs, so far outside price control have been brought in the price controlled category. Some of these were having a heavy annual turnover exceeding Rs. 10 crore. Eighty three drugs have been decontrolled. Many of these were having an insignificant annual turnover with a declining usage or negligible growth.

With price control on the 76 drugs mentioned in Schedule-I of the DPCO almost 50 per cent of the retail pharmaceutical market would be under price control. The associations of drugs manufacturers have been cautioned to advise all their members to exercise restraint and self discipline in regard to medicines going out of price control and to ensure that their prices are not raised unreasonably, so that Government is not constrained to excercise its powers to bring back these medicines under price control.

It is envisaged that the list of drug to be kept under price control will be reviewed periodically, based on the data to be collected in this regard. Substantial changes have been brought about so as to make the reporting system by way of forms and information required to be submitted periodically by the Industry to the Government, less cumbersome.

An important provision introduced is the stipulation of time limits of two months for deciding applications for price revision of formulations and four months for price fixation/revision of applications regarding bulk drugs. There is also a stipulation in the DPCO enjoining the Government to notify on an annual basis the norms relating to conversion costs, packing material costs and packing charges.

The new DPCO also provides for fixing of ceiling prices for commonly used packs of formulations based on price controlled drugs and these prices would be applicable to all manufactures and also the single ingredient formultions sold under generic name. The small scale sector will not be required to come for price fixation for these packs and they will be required to only adhere to the discipline of observing the ceiling prices. In regard to the other packs they would continue to enjoy, as before, exemption from price control on formulations.

A provision has also been added in the DPCO to allow for exemption from price control to a new bulk drug, which has not been produced elsewhere if developed through indigenous R&D. Further a provision has also been built to allow the of use funds collected in the Drug Equilisation Account for the purpose of promoting higher education and research in pharmaceutical sciences and technology and purposes incidental thereto.

The DPCO 1995 lays down a more transparent procedure for the working of the price control mechanism, which would be in the ultimate interest of the consumers as well as the manufacturers.

About 250 units in the organised sector, five of these in the public sector (IDPL, HAL, SSPL, BCPL and BIL) and six in the joint sector, and about 5,000 units in the small scale sector are engaged in the production of drugs. Of these, more than 100 are engaged in the production of bulk drugs.

Indian Drugs and Pharmaceuticals Limited (IDPL) incorporated under the Companies Act, 1956 on 5 April 1961, is a premier undertaking. The company has five plants including two wholly-owned subsidiaries; one each located at Rishikesh (Uttar Pradesh), Hyderabad (Andhra Pradesh), Gurgaon (Haryana), Madras (Tamil Nadu) and Muzaffarpur (Bihar). IDPL is a major producer of antibiotics like Pencillin-G, Tetracycline, Oxytetracycline from the basic stages. It is a leading producer of Vitamins again from the basic stages. In Madras Plant (subsidiary), the company produces sufgical instruments and formulations.

The company has a fully equipped Research Centre at the Synthetic Drug Plant in Hyderabad. IDPL has also set-up three subsidiary companies in collaboration with the respective state governments for production of quality pharmaceutical formulations. Rajasthan Drugs and Pharmaceuticals Limited (RDPL), Jaipur (Rajasthan); Uttar Pradesh Drugs and Pharmaceuticals Limited (UPDPL), Lucknow (Uttar Pradesh) and Orissa Drugs and Chemicals Limited (ODCL), Bhubaneswar (Orissa).

Hindustan Antibiotics Limited (HAL) incorporated on 1 March 1954, was the first public sector undertaking in the field of pharmaceuticals. The company set-up primarily with the objective of manufacturing Penicillin and other antibiotics. It also produces streptomycin, gentamycin, haymycin and aurofungin, besides formulations.

The company has recently entered into MOU for a joint venture tie-up with MAX-GB Limited for upgradation of the Pencillin-G production facilities. HAL has three subsidiary companies promoted in collaboration with the respective state government-Karnataka Antibiotics and Pharmaceuticals Limited (KAPL), Bangalore (Karnataka); Maharashtra Antibiotics and Pharmaceuticals Limited (MAPL), Nagpuir (Maharashtra) and Manipur State Drugs and Pharmaceuticals Limited (MSDPL), Imphal (Manipur).

There are three public sector undertakings engaged in the manufacture of drugs and formulations located at Calcutta (West Bengal). These were private sector comapnies, poineers again in their own field, but had been ailing over the year for various reasons. The management of these companies were taken over by the Central Government in terms of the Industries (Development & Regulation) Act 1951 and subsequently they were nationalised and new public sector companies were formed. Bengal Immunity Limited (BIL), Bengal Chemicals and Pharmaceuticals Limited (BCPL) and Smith Stanistreet Pharmaceuticals Limited (SSPL) are these three public sector undertakings with their main manufacturing activities concentrated in the State of West Bengal. BIl is one of the largest producers of SERA and vaccines toxoids.

It also produces other pharmaceutical formulations. BCPL with four manufacturing units, is the largest producer of anti-snake verum in India. It also produces chemicals like sulphuric acid, alum, chrome salts and home products like soaps, hair oil, perfumes etc. BCPL also produces herbal products. SSPL is engaged in the manufacture of pharmaceutical formulations.

The textile sector plays a vital role in the overall economy of the country. Textile exports account for over 30 per cent of the total exports from the country. The burgeoning growth in exports from the textile sector in the recent years has been one of the most striking features of India's economic development. The textile sector occupies a very prominent place in terms of employment generation.

The sectors like handloom, handicrafts, powerloom, sericulture and readymade * potential. The total employment in textile sector has risen from about 39 million during 1990-91 at about 47 million during 1994-95. The industry has witnessed a phenomenal growth during the last four decades. The spindleage increased from 11 million in 1951 to over 29.10 million and rotors from 45,000 in 1989 to 1,46,000 in 1994. The loomage, however has declined in the organised sector. Out of 1,227 cotton/man-made fibre textile mills, 187 mills are in public sector, 124 and 915 are in cooperative and private sectors respectively. Capacity utilisation in spinning sector of textile mills has increased from 69 per cent in 1985-86 to 84 per cent in 1993-94. However, the capacity utilisation in composite sector has declined from 62 per cent in 1985-86 to 54 per cent in 1993-94.

Research associations

Ahmadabad Textile Industry's Research Association, Ahmadabad, Bombay Textile Research Association, Bombay, South IndiaTextile Research Association, Coimbatore and Northern India Textile Research Association, Ghaziabad are four cotton textile research associations registered under the Societies Registration Act, 1860, and functioning under the adminstrative control of Ministry of Textile. The main objective of these institutions is to carry out research and render consultancy services (*i.e.* Quality Management Service-ISO 9000) to industry on various aspects of textile technology with a view to reducing the cost and improving the quality and durability of fabrics, reducing pollution, conserving energy and utilising waste, adopting new technology and improving the technologies in the decentralised handloom sector.

Silk and Art Silk Mills' Research Association (SASMIRA), Bombay is a textile research association registered under the Societies Registratiòn Act 1860 (XXI of 1860) of Maharashtra State. Its headquarters are located at Bombay. The SASMIRA's principal activities included research and development, provision of technical services, testing and training facilities in the fields of silk and art-silk. Man-Made Textile Research Association (MANTRA) established in 1981, occupies a status of the leading R&D and educational institution in

India today. as one of the National Textile Research Laboratory, MANTRA caters to multifarious needs of textile and allied industry at large. Though activities of MANTRA are primarily aimed at planned and healthy growth of decentalised textile industry of south Gujarat, its impact beyond south Gujarat is also significant.

Indian Jute Industries' Research Association (IJIRA), Calcutta, registered under the West Bengal Societies Registration Act, 1961, is an autonomous cooperative research organisation under the administrative control of the Ministry of Textiles, Government of India.

The objective of IJIRA is to promote research and other scientific work connected with the jute trade and industries allied with or accessory thereto, to establish and maintain laboratories and foster education of persons engaged in or likely to be engaged in the said trade and industry, to encourage discoveries, to examine and publish information regarding the nature and merits of inventions, improvements, materials and designs connected with the said trades or industries.

The Jute Industry in the country is traditionally export oriented. India ranks number one in raw jute and jute goods production and number two in export of jute goods in the world. Jute packaging materials are facing tough challenges from other low priced synthetic substitutes. As a measure to use jute in non-packaging sectors, Government has undertaken a number of steps for diversification.

The most significant aspect of the diversification programme is the UNDP assisted National Jute Programme under which an assistance of the order of US dollar 230 lakh from UNDP is being utilised by providing matching input from Government of India. A large number of projects covering the areas of raw jute production, R&D, product development, human resource development, and marketing are under imnplementation. To fulfil these objectives, the National Centre for Jute Diversification is being set up.

In the silk sector, Government has made an allocation of Rs. 901 crore for development of sericulture during Eighth Plan. The employment generation during this period is targeted at 10.50 lakh persons which would bring the accumulated employment under the sericulture sector to 65 lakh persons by 1997. The employment in silk sector during 1994-95 is anticipated to be 61 lakh persons as against 50 lakh persons in 1993-94. During 1994-95, the silk sector has exceeded its export target of Rs. 837.31 crore by 12.8 per cent.

The handloom industry is an important sector which provides employment to about 12 million people and contributes over 20 per cent of total cloth production. Production of handloom cloth also increased from 4,295 million sq mtr. during 1990-91 to 6,028 million sq. mtr. during 1994-95 showing an annual increase of about 10.1 per cent. In order to further increase production and generate additional employment opportunities in the handloom sector during 1992-93, a scheme was introduced to develop 3,000 handloom development centres and 500 quality dyeing units which will benefit 30 lakh weavers till September 1995.

Already 122 Handloom Development Centres and 45 Quality Dyeing Centres have been set up. An Integrated Village Handloom Development Scheme, project package scheme and National Silk Yarn Bank scheme have been launched between 1991-95 with an outlay of Rs. 63 crore and Rs. 20 crore respectively for the Eighth Plan period. A project on development of handloom products using jute fibre titled 'Development and Transfer for Technology for use of Jute Fibre in Handloom Textiles' was sanctioned by the Government during 1993-94 with an outlay of about Rs. 10.30 crore. Beside, a scheme for setting up jute handloom development centres has been introduced in January 1995.

Export of cotton handloom textiles amounted to Rs. 1,229 crore (US dollar 392 million) in April-December 1994 against Rs. 911 crore (US dollar 291 million) achieved in April-December 1993, thereby registering an increase of 34.8 per cent both in rupee and dollar terms.

In the decentralised powerloom sector which contributes over 70 per cent of the total cloth production, new scheme to set up computer aid designing centres (CADs) in the area of powerloom concentration has been inroduced. The aim of such centres is to upgrade the existing quality and design of cloth production by the decentralised powerloom sector so as to enable the powerloom fabric to compete in the international market in an effective fashion. Two such centres have been established at Sholapur (Maharashtra) and Coimbatore (Tamil Nadu). Remaining five centres are under process of being set up.

Textile exports, including handicraft, jute and coir, presently account for about 37 per cent of India's total exports as against of 35 per cent during the previous year. There has been a significant increase in exports from the textile sector * including jute, coir and handicrafts have grown from the level of Rs. 9,932 crore during 1990-91 to Rs. 31,644 crore during 1994-95.

The Final Act of the Uruguay Round of GATT negotiations has been signed by 111 countries at the Minsterial Conference in Marrakesh on 15 April 1994. The agreement on textile and clothing which forms a part of the Final Act, signalled the end of the Multi-Fibre Agreement (MFA) era, in which discriminatory restraints were put by the developed countries on the exports of textiles by developing countries like India. The World Trade Organisation has consequently come into existence w.e.f. 1 January 1995. During the next 10 years the multi-fibre agreement would be phased out and in the different stages the quotas will be removed. The agreement is expected to boost textile exports in the coming years.

In order to provide systematic training to our fashion designers and help them compete in the international market in an effective manner, in addition to the existing National Institute of Fashion Technology (NIFT) centre at New Delhi, five more new NIF centres have been opened at Bombay, Hyderabad, Calcutta, Madras and Gandhi Nagar.

Handicrafts constitute an important segment of the decentralised sector of our economy and provides employment to over six million artisans, roughly 1/5th of the total household industries scatteed throughout the country especially in rural and semi-urban areas.

The Office of the Development Commissioner for Handicrafts implements Plan schemes covering various areas like training, design, development, technology upgradation, market promotion, exhibition and publicity exports etc. Export of handicrafts including hand-knitted carpets during 1994-95 was recorded at Rs. 4,458 crore as compared to Rs. 3,360 crore during 1993-94. The employment in the handicraft sector has increased increased to 64.2 lakh persons during 1994-95.

Special programmes have been launched to promote embroidery, *zari* and *zardosi* costume jewellery and imitation jewellery for both in the domestic and international market as a measure to generate more employment opportunity for crafts people. Besides, a UNDP assisted programme has been undertaken to promote wood based handicrafts for exports. *Kaleen* label has been introduced by Carpet Export Promotion Council (CEPC) to be fixed on the carpets for export as a hall-mark of commitmemt towards complete eradication of child labour from the Indian carpet industry and contribution towards welfare of children and carpet weavers. A country-wide census has been launched for the first time to collect information about the handicrafts artisans. This will help in building up the data base for this sector.

The manufacture of all types of automobile vehicles is delicensed. There has been a significant growth in the production of automotive vehicles during 1994-95 as compared to that in 1993-94 * has been 1,94,999 as against 1,41,436 in 1993-94. Production of cars has gone up from 2,09,695 in 1993-94 to 2,64,007 in 1994-95. * The production of three-wheelers has gone up from 91,608 in 1993-94 to 1,27,532 in 1994-95. During 1994-95, the production of tractors was 1,62,900 as compared to 1,36,581 in 1993-94.

Sixty one units in the organised sector are manufacturing soap with an installed capacity of 6,60,772 tonnes per year. Production of soap in this sector was of the order of 3,40,366 tonnes during 1993-94 and 3,35,125 tonnes during 1994-95. There are 26 units in organised sector for manufacturing of synthetic detergents with an installed capacity of 6,05,000 tonnes per annum. Production of detergents was 3,07,738 tonnes during 193-94 and 3,09,738 tonnes during 1994-95.

Leather is a highly labour-oriented industry in India and has been identified as one of the major thrust areas for export. The export performance of leather sector has been improving considerably over the last 3-4 years. The value of export of leather and leather products went up from Rs. 3,693 crore during 1992-93 to Rs. 4,139.3 crore in

1993-94. In the year 1994-95, the export from this sector was to the tune of Rs. 5,000 crore (provisionally), showing a growth rate of nearly 18 per cent over the last year. Footwear in the leather sector has been identified as an area of extreme focus for exports and in 1993-94 leather footwear and footwear components valued at Rs. 1,481.3 crore have been exported.

A National Leather Development Programme (NLDP) with UNDP assistance of the order of US dollar 15.05 million and Government inputs of Rs. 28.43 crore is currently being implemented by the Government for integrated development of the leather industry through the selected institutions/agencies in the country. The duration of the programme is four years and it has started its operations in June 1992 in accordance with the Work Plan. The Programme covers, *inter-alia,* areas such as human resources development, improving support services, pollution control and enhancement of exports.

The Programme has already been able to establish linkages with some of the most reputed international organisations, such as AFPIC and MCT, Melbourne, in the areas of education and training. The Indian institutions have been able to upgrade the training systems for design and manufacture of footwear, garments and asserted leather products. The leather sector units in the country can directly seek assistance by the selected institutions on software.

The areas earmarked for assistance are human resource development, product development, development of supporting industries (components, machinery), marketing etc. A market research unit which has been established at Council for Leather Exports, Madras has commenced services. Resource Centre and Publication of bi-monthly *"World Leather Times"* has been started.

Chemical indusdry plays a pivotal role in the Indian economy. The Industry in India is well established and has witnessed rapid growth in the organic and inorganic sectors. The rate of growth of the chemical sector has consistently been higher than the average growth rate of the Indian industry. During the last decade (1981-82 to 1991), the industry has been averaging a growth rate of about 10 per cent per annum.

The present annual turnover in the chemical sector in India is estimated to be around Rs. 35,000-Rs. 40,000 crore which is likely to be doubled by the end of the century. In order to promote this highly technology oriented industry, a number of incentives have been given to promote development activities. With the liberalisation policy of the Indian economy, major reforms have been taken up in the Indian chemical industry.

Except for a small list of hazardous chemicals, all chemical items can be manufactured in India without requiring any industrial licensing. Even where licensing exists, the procedures have been streamlined. Entrepreneurs are, therefore, now free to set up chemical industries, by intimating to the Government through the Industrial Entrepreneurs Memorandum.

Development of organic chemical industry in India had started in April 1950, based on ethyl alcohol, manufactured from fermentation and distillation of sugarcane molasses and benezene available as a coke-oven by-product. At present, a substantial part of the industry is based on feedstock derived from petroleum. Basic organic chemicals like phenol, methanol, formaldehyde, acetone and acetic acid are manufactured in the country in substantial quantities. Major inorganic chemicals like soda ash, carbon black, calcium carbide, red phosphorous and potassium chlorates are all manufactured in the country and a position of near self-dufficiency has been achieved in all these chemicals. Alcohol producing industry was started in 1940 mainly to utilise molasses produced from fugar factories. With the growth of alcohol-based chemical industry in 1950's, production of alcohol has assumed importance in its own right.

Oil crisis has revived interest in the use of renewable feedstock like alcohol. It is mainly in India that a wide-range of organic chemical products are manufactured on a commercial scale with alcohol as the feedstock. The major downstream products made from ethyl alcohol (industrial alcohol) are acetic acid, acetic anhydride, acetone, butanol ethylacetate, polythene, styrene, PVC and synthetic rubber.

In keeping with the policy of economic liberalisation the price and movement control on molasses and alcohol have been removed with effect from 10 June 1993. This would ensure maximum utilisation of capacity in both the alcohol manufacturing sector and the sector utilising alcohol for downstream products like acetic acid, acetic anhydride etc.

Moreover, this is likely to improve the viablity of the sugar units who may be able to pay better prices for sugarcane to farmers. State governments are being persuaded for implementation of the policy of decontrol in their states.

In order to check undue increase in prices of industrial alcohol, customs duty on import of denatured alcohol has been reduced to 10 per cent with effect from 20 October 1993. Customs duty on molasses also has been reduced to 10 per cent with effect from 1 April 1995.

Dyestuff industry provides important inputs to many consuming industries contributing to the national economy. It is capable of meeting most of the local demands. In the organised sector, the industry is self-sufficient in terms of most of the inputs. There are around 50 units in the organised sector having a total installed capacity of 36,700 tonnes per annum against which the production achieved during 1993-94 was 31,100 tonnes.

The production for various classes of dyestuffs in 1994-95 is estimated to 31,600 tonnes. A large quantity of dyes and dye-intermediates is being exported and valuable foreign exchange being earned in this sector.

The industry contributes about 10 per cent of the total exports. The exports in the chemical sector have gone up from a level of around Rs. 1,600 crore in the year 1990-91 to around Rs. 3,600 crore in 1993-94, registering an increase of about 120 per cent.

Pesticides including insecticides, fungicides, weedicides, etc., are used extensively in agriculture and public health. The pesticide industry in india has made impressive progress and more than 60 technical grade pesticides are being successfully manufactured in the country. At present, more than 125 units are engaged in the manufacture of these technical grade pesticides and over 500 units are making pesticides formulations. As a result of the increased production of pesticides in the country, import of technical grade pesticides has come down considerably.

The estimated production of technical pesticides during 1994-95 is over 85,800 mt from an annual installed capacity of 1.25 lakh mt. As compared to this, the production during 1993-94 was around 85,600 mt.

In order to use the idle capacity available with pesticide units, the country has been able to enter the competitive field of export of pesticides. During 1992-93, the country has exported pesticides valued at Rs. 168.7 crore. This has increased to Rs. 261.24 crore during 1993-94. The courtry has started producing some new pesticides but continue to import their intermediates in the absence of technology for producing them.

Efforts are being made to acquire the right technology to manufacture intermediates for pesticides like Butachlor, Enosulfan etc. Till 1987-88, country was not able to export chemicals in larger quantities because of high cost of production of chemicals in India as compared to international prices. However, due to upgradation of technology and support given by the Government for exports, the Indian chemical industry have shown an impressive performance in the field of exports. During 1992-93, the export of chemical touched Rs. 3,475.5 crore.

There are two public sector units, namely, Hindustan Organic Chemicals Limited (HOCL) and Hindustan Insecticies Limited (HIL) in the chemical sector HOCL was incorporated in December, 1960 at Rasayani, Raigad district, Maharashtra, with the main objective of manufacturing chemical intermediates required for the manufacture of drugs, dyestuffs, rubber chemicals and laminates etc.

The company has two units; one each at Rasayani (Maharashtra) and Cochin (Kerala). Rasayani Unit produces organic grup of heavy chemical and intermediates such as nitrobenzene, hydrogen, aniline, sulphuric acid, acetic acid etc. Cochin unit produces phenol, acetone and propylene.

The company has floated a subsidiary company called Hindustan Fluocarbons Limited for setting up polytetraflurethylene (PTFE) plant in Medak district of Andhra Pradesh. HIL, incorporated in 1954, has at present three units at Delhi, Udyogamandal (Kerala) and

Rasayani (Maharashtra). The company als has a subsidiary Hyderabad and a factory at Kovur. HIL is engaged in the manufacture of DDT, BHC, malathion, endosulfan and butachlor, the five major pesticides used in the country. Monocrotophos Plant has also been commissional last year and is in operation.

Attainment of industrialisation over the last 48 years has been striking feature of Indian economic development process which was launched as a conscious and deliberate policy in the early fifties. In pursuance of this policy, large investment has been made in building up capacity over a wide spectrum of industries. Industrial production has made rapid strides in terms of variety, quality and quantity.

There has been a substantial diversification of industrial base during this period with the consequent ability to produce a very broad range of industrial goods. Self-reliance has been achieved in basic and capital good. Indigenous capabilities have now been established to the point of virtual self-sufficiency so that further expansion in various sectors such as mining, irrigation, power chemicals, transport and communication can be based primarily on indigenous equipment.

Process of industrialisation has also fostered entrepreneurship and development of a wide variety of technical, managerial and operative skills. Today, the country is in a position to provide consultancy services as well as managers, technicians and skilled workers for setting up industrial projects abroad.

The Industrial Policy Resolution of 1948 marked the beginning of the evolution of Indian Industrial Policy. The resolution not only defined the broad contours of the policy, it delineated the role of the State in the industrial development both as an entrepreneur and as an authority.

Successive policy resolutions also reiterated this basic tilt in favour of the public sector. The Industrial Policy Resolution of 1956 gave the public sector a strategic role in the economy. It categorised industries which would be the exclusive responsibility of state or would progressively come under state control and others. Earmarking the pre-eminent position to the public sector, it envisaged private sector co-existing with the State and thus attempted to give the policy framework flexibility.

The Industrial Policy initiatives undertaken by Government since July 1991 have been designed to build on the past industrial achievements and to accelerate the process of making Indian industry internatinally competitive. It recognises the strength and maturity of the industry and attempts to provide the competitive stimulus for higher growth. The thrust of these initiatives has been to increase domestic and external competition through extensive application of market mechanism and facilitating forging of dynamic relationships with foreign investors and suppliers of technology. The process of reform has been continuous.

As on 31 March 1993 there were 245 central public sector undertakings, comprising of eight in the construction sector, 72 in services and remaining 165 in the manufacturing. The number of CPSUs as indicated above exclude nine companies, six insurance companies and three financial institutions with Central Government investment but without direct responsibility of management.

The total capital employed in the 245 CPSUs increased from Rs. 1,179.91 billion in 1991-92 to Rs. 1,399.33 billion in 1992-93. The overall rate of return on capital employed in the PSUs also increased from 2.0 per cent in 1991-92 to 2.43 per cent in 1992-93.

The number of small scale units as at the end of 31 March 1994 were 2.38 million comprising of 1.77 million registered units and 0.61 un-registered. The overall production in the small scale sector during 1993-94 has been estimated to have reached Rs. 2,416.5 billion. The total value of exports of these units has been Rs. 177.85 billion in 1992-93.

Industrialization

India has made rapid strides in industrialization, and today is one of the ten most industrialized nations of the world. But industrialization, as in the rest of the world, has brought with it unwanted and unanticipated consequences. These include unplanned urbanization, pollution and risk of accidents. Industrialization moreover not only affects the immediate environment, but has consequences for a larger region whose resources get intimately tied to new industrial development.

Yet as the country continues to industrialize and new plants come up, some of the underlying issues remain. Dirty industries continue moving South. Hazardous chemicals are dumped or brought for reprocessing to developing countries. Often, in developed countries, different values are attached to human life in the North and in the South. Different standards are applied, and processes and factories being discarded in developed countries get relocated in the developing ones.

The Bhopal disaster, when methyl isocyanate crept into the houses of sleeping residents on the morning of 3 December, 1984, killing over 3,000 people and maiming countless others for life, brought many of these issues into sharp focus. It was a tragic testimony of just how much could go wrong. The hazardous side of industry became painfully apparent to countless people in India and abroad. It questioned location policies, safety requirements of industries, the responsibilities of North-based multinational corporations, the preparedness for dealing with disasters, citizens' right to know about the industrial process and the risks involved.

Near the industries, water and air pollution problems are very serious. Water pollution not only affects surface water but also groundwater. It is estimated that 70 per cent of India's surface water is seriously polluted and 80 per cent of the population does not have access to safe drinking water. For instance in Patancheru in Andhra Pradesh, over 60 factories—most of them chemical units—discharge their toxic wastes into freshwater streams. In Bichhri in Rajasthan, chemical effluents from textile and chemical industries pollute the waters of rivers and wells.

The health impact of such cases is serious and the incidence of cancer, lung and skin diseases, and deformities is high in these areas. While they are restricted in extent, air pollution levels are high in industrial areas. For instance the average levels of particulate matter in the four metropolitan cities exceeds 360 mg/m while the WHO standard is 150 mg/m.

Another concern relates to occupational health incertain industries. Asbestosis, byssinosis and pneumonoconiosis are some of the occupational diseases reported. Silicosis has been reported in mines and other industries.

Several central and state statues, such as the Industrial Development Act, the Labour Acts, the Factories Act and the Municipal Acts have environmental provisions in them. However it was the enactment of the Water (Prevention and Control of Pollution) Act, 1974, and the Air (Prevention and Control of Pollution) Act, 1981, which made these environmental factors the principal object of legislation. The Bhopal tragedy caused a surge in environmental legislation and an umbrella Environment (Protection) Act was passed in 1986. This covers hazardous activities in addition to pollution.

Under the Environment (Protection) Act, 1986, the Central Government is responsible for laying down procedures and safeguards for handling hazardous substances. Rules have been made for the manufactures, storage and import of hazardous chemicals, their management and handling, as well as for the manufacture, use, import and storage of micro-organisms and genetically engineered organisms. Radioactive waste disposal is controlled through a regulatory board managed by the Bhabha Atomic Research Centre. The Government has also established a Central Crises Group Alert System with a control room at New Delhi to deal with major chemical accidents in the country.

Many industries and large projects need environmental clearance. The State Pollution Control Boards monitor industrial areas. The Government of India has made it mandatory to assess the environmental impact of new large undertaking in the country. The impact assessment covers not only air, water and soil polluiton, but also damage to historical monuments, wildlife, forests, and to natural resources in general. Unique to India is the recently enacted Mandatory Public Liability Insurance which makes it imperative for units dealing with hazardous substances to take insurance cover against damage to health or property of the community in the vicinity of the industry.

Industrial location policy is a crucial element in determining the impact of industry on the environment. Unplanned industrial growth has in some cases led to industrail conglomerates and urban sprawl. This has often led to prime agricultural and forest land being diverted for urban and industrial use. Near forests, urban areas have led to deforestation. For certain industries, a two-stage clearance procedure has been adopted by the Ministry of Environment and Forests, considering the site specific nature.

While legislation today has enabled authorities to step in, this alone cannot lead to improved environment in and around industries. For this to happen public awareness, as well as awareness and concern among the decision-makers is required. Where people have been consicous they have protested and not let polluting industries spoil their environment. Where industries have been conscious they have got together and taken initiatives for effluent treatment. A typical example of joint efforts by industry in the safe disposal of effluents is the Baroda Effluent Channel in Gujarat, managed by the Gujarat Industrial Development Corporation.

There is urgent need to create widespread awareness. Towards this end the Ministry of Environment and Forests has made a beginning by introducing a scheme for an Ecomark to lable environment-friendly products. NGOs too have several programmes to create environmental consciouness. School programmes to involve students in environmental quality monitoring have begun.

But finally environmental factors will only be taken into account where alternatives are availabel. Today with Indai opening up its economy to greater internationl participation in the industrialization of the country, it si important to ensure that the best and cleansest technologies are available for htis growth, so that industrialization occurs with the minimum of negative consequences.

In a wide spectrum of industry and agriculture and the entire gamut of services, there has been great progress in the country during the post-Independence era. The growth in several sectors have indeed been spectacular and in several others it has been modest while in a few others outright dismal. On Monday, 10 November 1996, the foundation stone for the automobile plant of the Hyundai Motor Company of South Korea, was laid at Irungattukottai, some 40 km from Chennai. The plant involves an outlay of $ 700 million (around Rs. 2500 crore) in the first phase; and another $ 400 million (around Rs. 1440 crore) in the second phase.

A production capacity of around 100,000 passenger cars in the 1300 cc-1500 cc range is envisaged. The first car is expected to roll out of the assembly line by October 1998. Most importantly, HMC promises a 70 per cent indigenous content from the first car. Which means prospects for dozens of additonal collaboration arrangements and investments for the production of components. At full production, the turnover of HMC will be in the region of Rs. 6000 crore.

This is the third mega investment in the automobile sector involving outlays exceeding Rs. 1500 crore each. The other two relate to the Mahinndra-Ford India Ltd. project to produce passenger cars of similar capacity and in same medium segment; and by Ashok Leyland Ltd., planning to invest on facilities to expand capacity to 100,000 commercial vehicles.

In recent months total investments promised in Tamil Nadu exceed Rs. 5000 crore–an outlay that perhaps exceed all investments made on new projects in the first instance all through the past 50 years.

In all these areas, and in a wide spectrum of industry and agriculture and the entire gamut of services, there has been great progress through the years of Independent India. The growth in several sectors have indeed been spectacular and in several others, it had been modest; and in a few others outright dismal. The bench-making has been done both in regard to the potential offered by India and by developments in several other countries which started on industrialisation much later than we did. South Korea offers a ready example.

In looking at growth, over the last five decades, we can segment these into five distinct phase that roughly correspond with decennial slots.

In accordance with the prevailing thinking, the First Five year Plan stated that the objective of industrial planning was to make good the deficiencies in production of key industrial items and to initiated development, which would enable cumulative expansion of such basic production.

There was better appreciation in the First Plan of the need for coordination of industrial planning with the formulation of other economic policies, such as customs and excise tariff structure, import and export policy, investment and technology policy and monetary and financial policy. The Second Plan and later plans have been encreasingly concerned with the allocation of public resources and much less with indications and policies to direct the whole economy indesired directions.

The Industrial Policy Statement of 1973, inter alia, identified high-priority industries where investment from large industrial houses and foreign companies would be permitted. The Industrial Policy Statement of 1980 focussed attention on the need for promoting competition in domestice market, technological upgradation and modernisation. The policy laid the foundation for an increasingly competitive export base and for encouraging foreign investment in high priority technology areas. This found expression in the Sixth Five Year Plan, which emphasised the need for productivity to be the central concern in all economic and production activities.

Nevertheless the sector continued to provide the thrust for the development of heavy industries. In critical areas such as power, railways, coal, petroleum, steel and fertilisers, the public sector has been intensely involved in setting the pace of development.

Apart from public investments in basic industry and infrastructure, the expansion of the private sector in line with Plan objectives and priorities were greatly facilitated by financial institutions. An elaborate network of specialised development banking institutions with the Industrial Development Bank of India at the apex was established to help finance industrial investment in the private sector. These institutions, numbering over 50, have become the major source of long-term finance for the corporate sector.

As the statement on Industrial Policy, 1991 says, "These policies created a climate for rapid industrial growth in the country. Thus on the eve of the Seventh Five year Plan, a broad-based infractructure had been built up. Basic industries had been established. A high degree of self-reliance in a large number of items–raw materials, intermediates, finished goods—had been achieved. New growth centres of industrial activity had emerged, as had a new generation of entrepreneurs. A large number of engineers, technicians and skilled workers has been trained."

The Sixth Plan had achieved augmentation of new capacity more or less in consonance with the targets in alarge number of insdustries including, among others, aluminium, zinc, lead thermoplastics, yarn, petrochemical intermediates, electrical equipment, cement and consumer durables. However shortfall in production had taken place in some basic industries, such as steel, cement, non-ferrous metals, fertilisers and certain other industries, including textiles, jute manufactures, sugar, drugs and pharmaceuticals, commercial vehicles and railway wagons. Production targets were exceed in a few industries like machine toos, passenger cars, motor cycles and scooters, consumer electronics and communication equipment. Domestic imbalances resulting from shortfalls in production hasd to be corrected through imports of essential commodities, like steel, cement, fertilisers and sugar.

A technological thrust was given during the Plan period in certain industries in the engineering sector. The first 500 MW thermal generating unit was commissioned and the manufacture of 500 MW turbo generators and boilers had commenced. There has been a systematic upgradation of production technology for other equipment, needed by the power sector. The manufacture of equipment for 1350 tonnes per day fertiliser units and blast furnaces of 3200 cubic metres capacity for steel plants was being undertaken in the country. A strong base had been laid for the rapid development of the electronics sector.

The Seventh Plan recognised the need to consolidate on these strengths and to take initiatives to prepare Indian industry to respond effectively to the emerging challenges.

A number of policy and procedural changes which were introduced in 1985-86 aimed at increasing productivity, reducing costs and improving quality. Production capacity restrictions on the industries were gradually reduced and broad banding, which enabled a manufacturer to choose and produce any product mix which suited him in the context of the prevailing market conditions was introduced. In 1986, as against a policy of re-endorsement of existing capacity, the scheme of minimum economic scale of production was introduced with Letters of Intent prescribing a minimum economic size for a single unit. The accent was on opening the domestic market to increased competition and readying the industry to stand on its own in the face of international competition. The public sector was freed from a number of constraints and given a large measure of autonomy. The technological and managerial modernisation of industry was pursued as the key instrument for increasing productivity and improving competitiveness in the world.

As a result of the policies pursued since Independence, the long term trend of industrial growth for over forty years since 1950 is a trend annual growth of just over 6 per cent. This, says rakesh MOhan in an essay in Bimal Jalan's book on Indian Economy, "is quite an achievement, given the magnitude of distortions built into the system." He divides the growth record into three distinct periods: 7.7 per cent annual growth over the first three plan periods (1950-1965), four per cent annual growth over the holiday (1966-69) and the Fourth and Fifth Plan periods (1969-79), and finally the recovery to about 7.7 per cent growth over the Sixth and Seventh periods.

The period 1966-1980, says Mohan is effectively the dark period for Indian economy. This period encompassed a number of exogenous shocks: the devastating three-year drought of 1965-68, the aftermath of increased defence espenditures resulting from 1962 was with China and two wars with Pakistan, the oil price shocks of 1973 and 1979, and the downturn in the availability of foreign resources. During this period, the Indian economy was constantly struggling to adjust.

As a result of policy changes, the composition of

Indian industry had undergone great transformation. At Independence, the consumer goods industry accounted for almost half of all industrial production. In 1991 such industries accounted for only about 20 per cent. In contrast, capital goods production was less than 4 per cent of total industrial production. In 1991, it had gone up to 24 per cent. Similarly basic goods share had increased from 20 per cent to 40 per cent.

As per the quick estimates of the Index of Industrial Production, the overall growth of industrial production during April-June 1996 was 8.5 per cent over the corresponding period of 1995 with the following sectoral contributions. As per the use based classificaton of industries, the overall growth has been broad based. After being relatively sluggish in the last two years, Intermediate Goods have recorded a growth of 11.9% in April-June 1996.

Industrial performance based on the production of 172 industries which together have a weight of 88% of IIP indicate a growth of 9.98 per cent in April-June, 1996. There has been deceleration in the growth of certain core sectors such as electricity, crude petroleum, steel, fertilizers, ferro alloys, jute manufacturers etc.

The first five months of the current financial year witnessed a sharp drop in the growth rate of infrastructure industries to 3.5% from 7.8% for the corresponding period of 1995-96. Amongst the industries that declined are: crude petroleum at (-)10.4% from 7.2%, electricity at 2.4% from 8.2% and saleable steel at 4.6% from 8.5%.

The performance of six Infrastructure Industries which is a critical indicator of the overall health.

The Office of Economic Adviser (OEA) also collects advance information on the production of 24 selected industries which have a weight of around 50% in the IIP. According to the information available, these industries have recorded a growth of 5.8% during April-July, 1996.

As per the information provided by CMIE, the corporate sector recorded a robust 22% growth in sales during 1995-96. This was particularly impressive because it comes after an unsually high increase of 23% recorded during 1994-95. The growth was reasonably well spread over major industry groups In particular, the automobiles group, the chemicals sector and machinery industry performed exceptionally well.

About a quarter of the companies surveyed recorded sales growth rates less than 10%. At the same time, a little over a quarter of the companies recorded growth rates of more than 50%. Growth was mostly concentrated amongst companies with a size of Rs.75 crore to Rs.100 crore in terms of sales.

Interest payment by the corporate sector increased at a faster pace (nearly 24%) compared to the growth in sales. High interest cost during the year adversely affected most companies except the very large ones. However, the higher interest cost did not dampened sales growth in 1995-96.

According to the report of the RPG Foundation, the performance of non-finance companies was the highest during 1995-96 when compared to the other years in the 90s. Despite the liquidity crunch, the companies fared well mainly due to high and relatively inelastic demand for industrial goods, increased velocity of circulation of money, better inventory management and a decline in the incremental capital output ratio of the corporate sector. Thus despite paying a higher interest of at least 3% points more, there was a marginal improvemeant in the average rate of capital employed and the net profitability of the corporate sector.

Advance indications of the corporate performance for the first half of 1996-97 are now becoming available. These indicate a slow down in sales growth to around 9 per cent compared to over 24 per cent in the previous year. With inflation at around 5 per cent, real sales growth is around 4-5 per cent. Inventory levels are also increasing and with that interest burden. The liquidity crunch witnessed in 1995-96 and resultant high interest rates are affecting corporate investment in the current year.

In a period of weak sales growth, one normally excepts a high inventory holdings. However, continued high interest rates in last few years has resulted in better inventory management and the inventory levels have been declining continuously. These were around 20 per cent of sales in 1995-96. Even a significant increase in inventory holdings will not make much difference to the production levels.

NCAER regularly conducts a Survey of Industrial Confidence. According to the latest information available the business confidence index for August has sharply declined indicating that second half of 1996-97 may be even worse than the first half. Psychologically the corporate sector is now excepting a slow down in industrial activity and the inertia of this deceleration may result in a slow down greater than what economic fundamental may indicate.

Power sector

Power generation during 1995-96 at 380.1 billion kwh recorded a growth of 8.3 per cent over 1994-95. Total generation of power during April-November, 1996 at 257.2 billion kwh, compared to 248.7 billion kwh during April-November, 1995 recorded a growth of 3.4 per cent. While thermal and nuclear generation went up by 6.5 per cent and 4.1 per cent respectively, hydro generation declined by 7.7 per cent. Owing to the low Plant Load Factor (PLF) of thermal plants, heavy Transmission and Distribution (T&D) losses and other operational and technical inefficiencies, full benefits are not being derived even from existing capacities.

Thermal plants at present account for 74 per cent of total power generation and hydro electricity plants 24 per cent, with the balance 2 per cent being generated by nuclear plants. The installed capacity of power generation as on March 31, 1996 was 83,288 MW. During the first 4 years of the 8th plan (1992-97) capacity addition has been 14,799 MW as against the 8th Plan target of 30,858 MW. About 12 per cent of the total capacity addition during the first four years has been accounted for by hydro and the remaining by thermal units.

Nearly half of the addition to capacity occurred in the Central Sector. 4.25 per cent was accounted for by the State Sector and the rest in the Private Sector. While the Central Sector has achieved 57.0 per cent of the 8th Plan, the State and Private Sectors achieved 42.3 per cent and 41.9 per per cent respectively. During the period (April-November) of the current year (1996-97) there has been a capacity addition of 53.460 MW of which 105.60 MW is in the private sector.

Several reasons have been identified for slippages in capacity creation in the Central and State sector. These include paucity of funds, delay in placement of order for main plant and equipment, delay in supply of equipment by suppliers, procedural delays in land acquisition, non-resolution of inter-state disputes, problems due to disturbed site conditions at some of the projects, unresolved issues in fuel linkages, suspension of work due to contract failures and resettlement and rehabilitation problems. Another important reason for slippages, particularly in State sector projects has been that the States saw the announcement of policy for private participation as an opportunity to cut back on their involvement in generation projects. As a result many projects that were scheduled for commissioning through the State sector resources have not been provided adequate funds for timely completion.

The PLF is an important indicator of operational efficiency of thermal power plants. The average PLF in the Central PSUs in 1995-96 and in April-November, 1996 was appreciably higher than that achieved by the State Electricity boards (SEBs). The low capacity utilisation of thermal power plants of the SEBs is largely due to deficiencies in management and operation, lack of proper maintenance and non-availabilty of coal of appropriate quality. There were wide inter-state variations in the average PLF of thermal plants and the average PLF in the case of Eastern and North Eastern regions continued to be much lower than the all India average during. 1996-97.

An action plan has been drawn up to improve the performace of the power sector in a phased manner. This involves short-term, medium-term and long-term measures and covers both the physical and financial aspects of generation, transmission and distribution of power. Short-term measures include overhaul and maintenance (O & M) of boileers and optimal operation of the regional grids. Significant improvements in the PLF of thermal power stations can be effected through medium-term measures like proper maintenance planning. In the long-term, the availability factor of the older thermal power plants can be improved by appropriate renovation and modernisation (R & M) programmes.

In the power sector, SEBs are responsible for distribution to all end users other than a small segment under the purview of privae distribution companies. As a result, in principle, all the electricity generated is to be sold to SEBs. But the financial condition of SEBs, though it differs from one state to the other, is fragile in most cases. The magnitude of losses incurred by SEBs over the period 1990-91 to 1994-95.

The industry and agriculture sectors continued to be the two most important categories of consumers in terms of their relative shares, with SEB electricity charges set at much below the unit cost for the agricultural sector and above the unit cost for the industrial sector. In none of the SEBs does unit revenue realisation from the agricultural sector cover even a reasonable fraction of the unit average cost for the SEB, and this is leading to heavy financial losses.

The commercial losses of SEBs which, in absolute terms, were a little over Rs. 4.000 crore in 1991-92, have shot up over a five year period to Rs. 10,941 crore in 1996-97 (RE). The hidden subsidy for the agriculture and domestic sectors has increased from Rs. 7,248 crore in 1991-92 to Rs. 19,227 crore in 1996-97 (RE) and is projected to further go upt to Rs 21,580 crore in 1997-98. Introduction of proposed national minimum agricultural tariff of 50 paise/kwh, even if implemented, will leave uncovered a substantial proportion of the subsidy provided to the sector.

In addition the SEBs have continued to suffer from high T & D losses, which stood at 21.8 per cent in 1992-93, have come down marginally to 20.9 per cent in 1994-95. These figures are very high when compared with the international average of less than 10 per cent for the advanced countries of the world. A reduction in T & D losses by 1 per cent would result in saving of capacity of about 800 MW at present day consumption. These T & D losses are due to the sparsely distributed loads over large rural area, substancial amount of energy sold at low voltage level. under-investment in the power distribution systems, inadequated billing and high pilferage. Inherent losses in conductors and equipment can be brought down through system improvement schemes and the pilferage and theft of energy can be reduced through appropriate administrative measures.

Restoration of the financial health of SEBs and improvement in their operational performance continue to remain the most crucial issues in the power sector. In terms of Section 59 of the Electricity (Supply) Act, 1948, SEBs are required to earn a minimum rate of return (ROR) of 3 per cent on their net fixed assest in service, after providing for depreciation and interest charges. This provision was to become operative from the accounting year of 1985. However the SEBs are yet to comply with this statutory stipulation. Whereas in 1992-93, the number of SEBs with a positive ROR were 11, there were only 6 such SEBs in 1994-95. Similarly, as against 5 SEBs with negative ROR in 1992-93, the number of such SEBs have increased to 9 in 1994-95.

There were only 3 SEBs with a ROR Return of more than 3 per cent in 1994-95. The managerial and financial inefficiencies in the state sector utilities have in turn adversely affected future capacity addition and system improvement programme. On the one hand, the SEBs do not have enough resources to finance future programmes and, on the other, their ability to raise investible funds from alternate sources in limited due to their poor financial and commerical performance.

Diagnostic studies aimed at reform and restructuring of the State power sector with a view to improving its physical and financial performance have been initiated in several States namely Haryana, Uttar Pradesh, Rajasthan, Gujarat and Andhra Pradesh. Similar studies are being considered in Kerala and Karnataka. the State of Orissa has provided the framework for reform envisaged through the enactment of a reform legislation, namely "The Orissa Reform Act, 1995" made effective from 1.495. A few other states are also considering similar steps.

The net budgetary support to the Central PSUs under the Ministry of Power as a proportion of the approved plan outlay has been declining steadily over the years. It stood at about Rs. 719.5 crore in 1996-97 and this amounted to only 10.6 per cent of total plan outlay. Owing to the decline in budgetary support, the central PSUs have to mobilise resources through internal and extra budgetary resources (IEBR). During 1995-96, the PSUs wer able to mobilise resources amounting to Rs. 3,593.8 crore as against the approved allocation of Rs. 4,326.9 crore under IEBR. Against the total plan outlay of Rs. 6,923.5 crore for the year 1995-96, the actual utilisation (Provisional) is of the order of Rs. 5,760.3 crore. During 1996-97, the IEBR component constitutes Rs. 4,565.5 crore (67 per cent) of the total approved plan outlay of Rs. 6,790.3 crore.

In view of the paucity of resources with Central/ State PSUs as well as the SEBs and the need to bridge the gap between the rapidly growing demand for the supply of electricity, there is a policy to encourage greater investment by private enterprises in the power sector. This policy, which has the objective of mobilising additional resources for capacity addition in power generation and distribution had been formulated in 1991, and is currently under implementation. The policy to invite private participation in the power sector also covers areas of transmission and distribution besides generation. The response to the policy has been expressed in putting up more than 124 power projects (requiring clearance of the Central Electricity Authority) for a total capacity of 67281 MW and involving and investment of about Rs. 2,46,472 crore. In addition, there are several projects (MOU/LOI projects costing up to Rs. 100 crore and Projects awarded through competitive bidding and costing up to Rs. 1000 crore) which are being set up by the private sector with the approval of the concerned State Government itself

In order to make the policy more attractive, the tariff notification has been amended twice to offer an assorment of incentives to investors. The Government has revised the hydro tariff guidelines to boost private investment in hydro-electric projects. To bring about private investment in the renovation, modernisation and upgradation of old power plants, the Government has finalised the policy and the guidelines have been issued. The Govenment has also taken steps to encourage captive/co-generation plants by industries. In order to encourage short gestation period projects, the Government has decided to permit setting up of power projects based on heavy fuel oils such as napha, heavy petroleum stock (HPS), low sulphur heavy stock (LSHS), heavy furnace oil (HFO), furnace oil (FO) and natural gas, wherever available, as primary fuel.

Under the current structure, the Independent Power Producers (IPPs) generally sell powers to SEBs which distribute power. Since most SEBs are financially distressed, the security package for an IPP is crucial to the success of a power project.

As an initial measure to attract private capital into the power sector, the Government of India had agreed to extend counter-guarantees to State-guarantees for the SEB's payment obligations to generating companies in respect eight fast track private power projects. This was a confidence building measure necessary for the initial batch of projects. Though these guarantees increase the comfort-levels of lenders in the initial phases, extensive use of these measures can lead to large contingent liabilities that would over-expose the concerned governments. Other options for securing the revenue stream of IPPs include Escrow Accounts, Guarantees from Multilateral Development Banks and Direct sale to high tension customers. The status of these eight fast track IPPs for which counter-guarantees have been or will be extended. Most of these projects are expecting financial and technical closure soon.

To facilitate the setting up of large sized thermal/ hydel power plants in the country, and to derive economies of scale, projects having a capacity of 1000 MW or above and supplying power to more than one stae are being considered as Mega projects. The SEBs and the State Government have been advised to introduce a more competitive element in the process of selection of selection of developers and award of projects. A notification was issued in October, 1995 enhancing concurrence of the Central Electricity Authority from Rs. 100 crore to Rs. 400 crore in the case of generating companies. The limit has been further enchanced to Rs. 1000 crore in September, 1996.

Capative power generation units in industry are used to supplement the power drawn from the grid and as a stand-by in case of power cuts. As of now, the country has an installed captive generation capacity of more than 10,000 MW. The policies relating to captive generation have also been liberalised. A 50 per cent thershold level has been prescribed for the industry's own consumption from the capative unit, and capacity in excess of this level can be sold to the grid.

In view of the widening gap between demand and supply and the huge capital cost involved in the installation of new power plants, a movement has been launched to make consumers aware of the need to save energy. Moreover, the Government is vigorously promoting energy accounting and monitoring systems. Energy audits have been carried out in a number of industrial units to identigy energy saving opportunities and eliminate wastage and to ensure that industries adopt the recommendations ofthese energy audits. Steps have been taken to improve the efficiency of domestic electrical appliances and agricultural pump sets and to promote the usage of fuel efficient engines and motors in both agricultural and transport sectors. Efforts are also being made to encourage co-generation of electricity in such industries as sugar, paper, cement, pertrochemicals and fertilisers.

The Government is working on a three-pronged strategy to overcome the existing structural constraints, technical inefficiencies and financial constraints. These include short and long-term measures to meet the power supply situation, encourage greater doses of private capital in power generation and facilitate reforms and restructuring in the state utilities. The Chief Ministers of different States met on 16th October, 1996 and 3rd December, 1996 to discuss and deliberate upon issues pertaining to the power sector. In the course of these deliberations a national consensus evolved for improving the performance of the power sector in a time bound manner and a Common Minimum National Action Plan for Power was adopted.

North-eastern Electric Power Corporation Limited (NEEPCO) was constituted in 1976 under the Companies Act to harness the power potential of the north-eastern region through planned development of power generation projects. The Corporation is responsible for operation and maintenance of the 150 mw Kopili-Hydro Electric Project which was commissioned in June/July 1988. The Corporation is presently executing the following projects: (i) Doyang Hydro-Electric Project (75 mw), Nagaland; (ii) Ranganadi Hydro electric Project (405 mw), Arunachal Pradesh; (iii) Assam Gas Based Project (291 mw), Assam; (iv) Kopali Ist stage extension Project (100 mw), Assam; and (v) Agartala Gas Turbine Project (84 mw), Tripura.

Tehri Hydro development Corporation limited (THDC) was incorporated as a joint venture public sector undertaking under the Companies Act, 1956 on 12 July 1988 for execution of Tehri Hydro Power Complex at Tehri (Garhwal) in Uttar Pradesh. The Corporation with equity participation of Government of India and Uttar Pradesh in the ratio of 75:25 (for power component of Tehri Complex) will also execute other hydro-electric projects with the consent of the state government. It has an authorised share capital of rs. 1,200 crore.

Tehri Hydro Power Complex with a generation capacity of 2400 mw comprises: (a) Tehri Dam and Hydro Powder Plant, 1000 mw (4 × 250 mw); (b) Tehri Pumped Storage Plant 1000 mw (4 × 250 mw); (c) Koteshwar Dam 400 mw (4 × 100 mw) and (d) Associated Transmission System (800 kv/400 kv) for evacuation of power. The project will generate 6,322 million units of energy per year and will provide additional irrigation facilities to 2.7 lakh hectare, besides stabilising existing irrigation facility in 6.04 lakh hectare of land.

Natpha Jhakri Power Corporation (NJPC) was incorporated on 24 May 1988 to plan, promote, organise, execute, operate and maintain hydro-electric power projects in the Satluj rover basin in Himachal Pradesh. The authorised share capital of NJPC is Rs. 1,000 crore and equity loan ratio is 1:1. Satluj river, which originates from lake Mansarover has so far been harnessed. The Nathpa Jhakri HEP is the first project taken up by the Corporation as a joint venture of Government of India and Government of Himachal Pradesh both sharing the cost of the project in the ratio of 3:1 respectively. The Nathpa Jhakri Hydro-electric project with an installed capacity of 1,500 mw is being executed by NJPC with partial assistance of 437 million US dollar from World Bank. The project is located in Kinnaur and Shimla districts of Himachal Pradesh and envisages to harness the hydro power potential in the upper reaches of river Satluj in the form of a run-of-over scheme.

Four major contracts in respect of the civil works pertaining to the Dam & Desilting Complex, the Head Race Tunnel and Surge Shaft, the Power House complex have been awarded in June - September, 1993 to three International Consortia each of whom has an Indian construction company as its partner. The work on these contracts has picked up momentum.

Damodar Valley Corporation (DVC), the first multi-purpose river valley project of the Government of India, was set up on 7 July 1948 under DVC Act (XIV of 1948) for the unified development of Damodar Valley region spread over the states of Bihar and West Bengal. DVC's objectives include flood control and irrigation, power generation and distribution, soil conservation, social and economic well-being of the people of Damodar Valley region. DVC's main projects include four dams at Maithon, Panchet, Tilaiya and Konar, four thermal power statin at Bokaro 'A', Bokaro 'B', Chandrapura and Durgapur and three hydel stations at Maithon, Panchet and Tilaiya and also one gas turbine station at Maithon.

DVC has practically become synonymous with power generation and distribution by supplying power to coal, mines, steelplants, railways and other big industries, besides state electricity boards of Bihar and West Bengal. Installed capacity of DVC in 1994-95 was 2,146 mw comprising of 1,920 mw thermal, 144 mw hydel and 82.5 mw bygas turbine. Total length of transmission lines of DVC runs over 5,000 circuit km. During the last financial year DVC generated 6,912 mw of power.

Bhakra Beas Management Board administers, maintains and operates the largest multi-purpose river valley project in the country to meet the irrigation and power needs of northern region which consitutes the granary of the nation and contributes over 90 per cent of foodgrains for the Public Distribution System. The installed capacity of power plants is 2,705 mw and the Board manages the operation of about 574 ckt km of 40 kv lines and 2,998 ckt km of 220 kv lines. The achievements during the last five years reflect complete harmony/congruence of individual and organisation goals' thereby creating synergy and a result oriented approach.

The National Power training Institute (formerly Power Engineers Training Society) was formed in 1980 as an autonomous body. The Institute is responsible for coordinating training programmes of the various state electricity boards, power stations, etc., and supplementing these with its own traiing activities. It has four regional power training institutes at Neyveli, Durgapur, Badarpur (New Delhi) and Nagpur. These institutes conduct regular induction courses, in-service refresher and short-term courses, on=job and on-plant training programmes for power engineers, operators and technicians of thermal power stations, state electricity boards, etc. A simulator installed at the training institute at Badarpur (New Delhi) Provides training to engineers and operators of 210 mw thermal units.

Central Power Research Institute (CPRI), which was set up in 1960 as a subordinate office under the erstwhile Central Water and Power Comission (Power Wing), was reorganised as a society under the Karnataka Societies

Act, 1960 w.e.f. January 1978. CPRI functions as national laboratory for applied research in the field of electric power engineering. While CPRI has its units located at Bhopal, Hyderabad, Koradi, Muradnagar and Thiruvananthhapuram, the main complex of its laboratories is at Bangalore. The Institute is an apex body for research and development in the power sector and conducts tests of electrical apparatus in accordance with national/international standards so as to meet fully the research and testing needs of electrical, transmission and distribution equipment. It also serves as a national testing and certification authority for transmission and distribution equipment. The Institute possesses highly sophisticated laboratories comparable to those in development countries.

Energy Management Centre (EMC) was established by the Government of India in April 1989 to act as a focal point for exchange of experience among energy institutes within India and as a centre for information, research and training activities in the energy field based on cooperation between India and the European Communities. The activities of EMC are : (i) to develop a national energy database by collecting and analysing data on energy supply, demand and infromation on prices; (ii) identify barriers for improving energy efficiency and propose appropriate incentives and other measures to overcome them.

These would include recommendations for assistance with capital investment, taxes duties and other financial incentives; (iii) to review laws and regulations that have an impact on energy consumption and propose modifications and formulate suitable policies and actions; (iv) to suggest introduction of standards, labels and setting of consumption targets; (v) to organise public infromation and promotional and promotional campaign on an on-going basis; and (vi) to organise specific promotional campaigns for the main energy consuming sectors (industry, transport, agriculture, commercial and government buildings). The Centre also provides technical assistance in the field of energy efficiency and fuel sectors; promotes energy audits enterprises and provides recommendations to improve energy efficiency and fuel substitution; and * initiates follow-up actions where needed; and organises training for energy managers and equipment operators.

The investment in Research and Development. (R & D) has increased from a paltry Rs. 20 crore in the First Five Year Plan. Presently there are 214 universities, 400 national laboratories and 1300 in-house R & D centres in the industrial sector. Several Science & Technology departments have been set up in the areas of environment, non-conventional energy resources, bio-technology, ocean development, industrial research, space, atomic energy, defence, health, agriculture and electronics.

Identification and promotion of priority areas in R & D is done by Science an Engineering Research Council (SERC) set up under the Department of Science & Technology (DST). DST supports 12 autonomous research insitutions as well, for furthering research work in several discipline. Technology Information, Forecasting and Assessment Council (TIFAC) has been set up for generating technology forecasting and technology assessment documents and enabling a technology information system that is interactive and nationally accessible.

Industrial research in several diverse fields of scientific activity is being undertaken through a network of 40 laboratories and 81 field stations set up by the Council for Scientific and Industrial Research (CSIR). In the field of bio-technology, more than 24 specialised R &

D centres have been developed for pursuing state-of-the-art research. Identical efforts for promoting new avenues of research are being undertaken in the field of ocean development as well.

The Union Budget for 1996-97 has taken various measures to promote R & D facilities. A matching one time grant has been awarded to CSIR and the Indian Council of Agricultural Research (ICAR) for modernisation of laboratories and institutes. The Technology Development and Application Fund created in 1995-96 has been proposed to be strengthened by Rs. 30 crore. A Five Year Tax Holiday under Section 80-IA of the Income Tax Act has been allowed to companies exclusively create for participation in R & D activities. The existing procedure for awarding weighted deduction under Section 35(2AA) of the Income Tax Act on sums paid for scientific research to a National Laboratory or a University or an IIT has been amended, by deleting the condition of approval by an outside body. In order to encourage R & D efforts, goods developed and patented in India and concurrently in specified countries have been exempted from levy of excise duty for a period of 3 years. The exemption procedure for customs duty on import of equipment and consumables for R & D institutions has been rationalised as well.